Gregor, Arthur S.

Lifestyles

LIFE STYLES

ARTHUR S. GREGOR

LIFE

an introduction

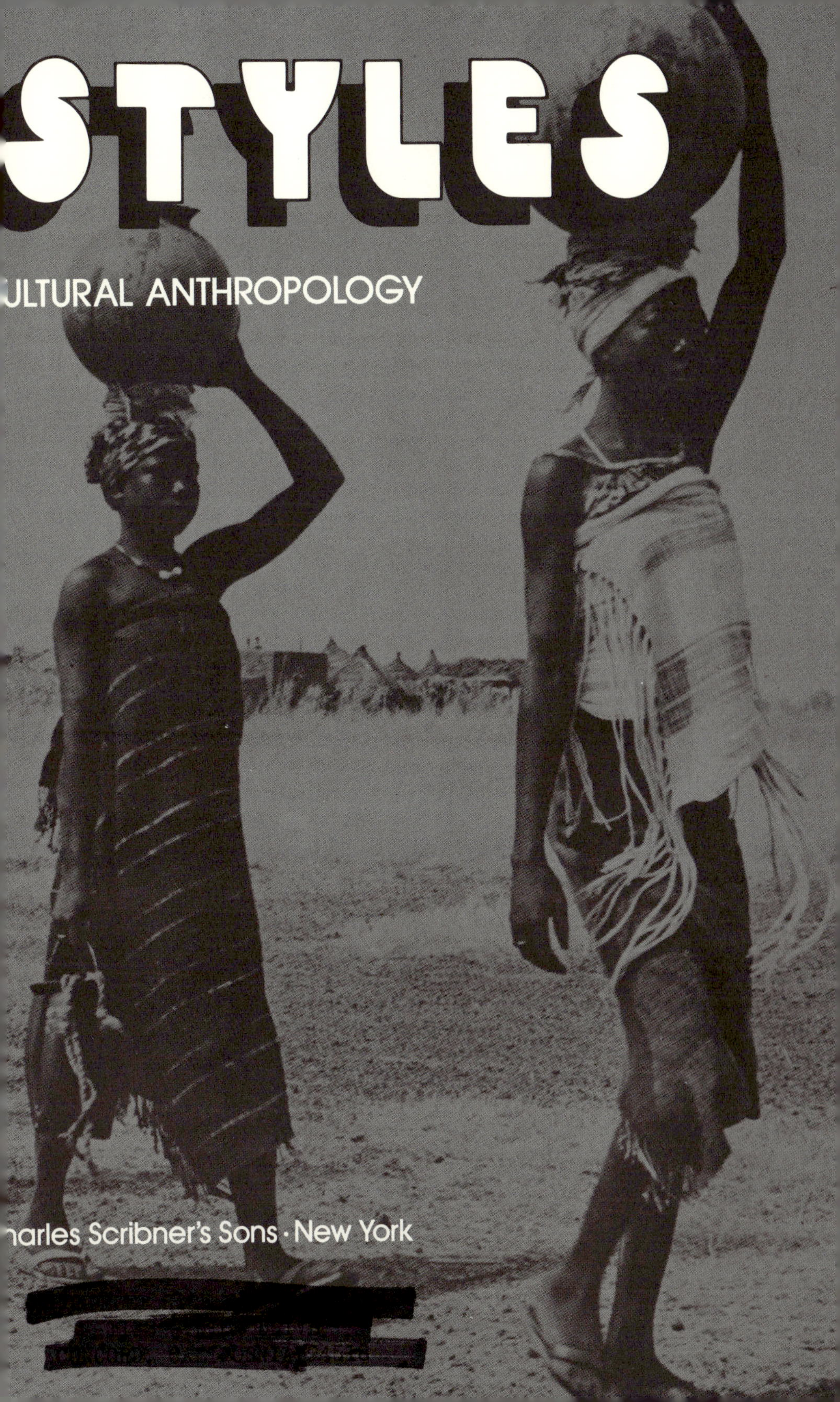

STYLES

ULTURAL ANTHROPOLOGY

harles Scribner's Sons · New York

For

FRANCES

and

LESTER

Library of Congress Cataloging in Publication Data
Gregor, Arthur S.
Lifestyles : an introduction to cultural anthropology.
Bibliography: p. 232
Includes index.
SUMMARY: Explores the diversity of human behavior in such areas as puberty, sexual behavior, family relations, and the status of women.
1. Ethnology—Juvenile literature. [1. Ethnology]
I. Title.
GN333.G73 301.2 78-3416
ISBN 0-684-15599-0

1 3 5 7 9 11 13 15 17 19 V/C 20 18 16 14 12 10 8 6 4 2

Printed in the United States of America

acknowledgments

IN A traditional, so-called primitive society it is the destiny of the young to learn from the elders. In our own ever-changing Western society it is sometimes the good fortune of the elders to receive instruction from the younger generation. With delight I acknowledge my indebtedness to my son, Thomas Gregor, who, despite the demands of a very exacting schedule, found the time to give me good counsel and help steer me clear of some of the pitfalls that lie in wait for the unwary author.

I am also pleased to acknowledge my indebtedness to these individuals from whom I have quoted briefly: Art Buchwald, Jimmy Carter, John Crane (now Minister of Jefferson Unitarian Church, Golden, Colorado), Erik Erikson, Clark Kerr, John Lennon, Claude Lévi-Strauss, Ralph Linton, Margaret Mead, Robert C. Petersen, Rosalyn S. Yalow.

—A.S.G.

Grateful acknowledgment is made to the following for permission to reproduce illustrative material:

Army News Features, p. 120; Australian Information Service, p. 141; Australian Tourist Commission, 168 (left); Canadian Consulate General, 64, 132;

Canadian Government Travel Bureau, 212; Consulate General of Israel, 49, 58, 76; Consulate General of Japan, N.Y., 60, 89, 147; FAO or FAO/WFP, 38, 72, 92 (top), 96, 164, 170, 178 (top), 223, 224; Thomas Gregor, 102, 110 (top), 125, 139, 216, 217; Information Service of India, 67; Japan National Tourist Organization, 162, 166; NASA, 69; National Film Board of Canada, 141, 181, 197; United Nations, 5 (upper and lower left and right), 9, 12, 20, 36, 40, 54, 63, 79, 90, 92 (bottom), 95 (top), 98, 108 (top and bottom), 110 (bottom), 113, 114, 117, 119, 137, 168 (right), 178 (bottom), 184, 197, 226; UNESCO, 33, 95 (top), 118, 159, 201; UNICEF, xii, 63 (top); US Navy, 115; WHO, x, 24, 28, 34, 150, 186, 189, 194, 205.

Identification for photographs not identified with captions: Title page, Women in village in Upper Volta, Africa, going for water; p. xiv, Vietnamese infant; 12, Young girl, Senegal, Africa; 24, "Flower child" of the 1960s, United States; 60, Japanese family; 102, Indonesian children; 120, American soldiers in the Vietnam War; 132, Old Indian woman, British Columbia; 150, Religious procession, New York; 194, American youth in the 1960s; 212, Tribal dancers, Banff, Canada.

Anthropology (Greek: *anthrōpos,* man; -logy, study) is the study of humans and their life ways. A wide-spectrum science, it is divided into a number of specialized fields:

Physical anthropology includes the study of (1) human evolution, (2) human races, and (3) physical differences among the people of the earth.

Cultural anthropology, the study of human cultures, includes (1) linguistics, which deals with the origin and development of languages, especially those that have no system of writing; (2) archaeology, which reconstructs the human past through excavation of artifacts and remains; (3) ethnography, which describes specific societies; and (4) ethnology, which analyzes and compares the ways of living, or the life styles, of different peoples.

contents

preface

FROM the time of Marco Polo explorers and travelers have arrived home from distant lands with fascinating tales about the varied ways of living of the inhabitants of the earth. Whether in the Far East, the Amazon, the Arctic, or on South Pacific islands, these wanderers came upon different peoples, all of whom had their own manner of thinking, feeling, and behaving, as well as their own language, institutions, and customs. Though the human race was one, there was no one way of life. Rather there were thousands of designs for living, so distinct that we may say that each was a separate culture or life style.

The diversity of behavior among the peoples of the earth is enormous. Consider gestures, for example. In some human communities bending the index finger toward oneself means "Come here," in others, it means "Go away." Or take responses toward pain. Western people try to keep away from anything that causes pain, but fire walkers in the South Seas and elsewhere deliberately tread on beds of white-hot coals. Or attitudes toward animals: In India cows are permitted to wander through city streets; in Western countries dogs often run freely in the home, a practice visitors from India find abhorrent. Or the expression of aggression: Middle-class American parents teach children not to hit. "Talk it over first," they say. Other peoples encourage aggressive behavior. Among the Yanomamö Indians who live on the border of Brazil and Venezuela, a father deliberately goads his four-year-old son into fury until the child in desperation strikes him across the face. Then instead of punishing the child, the father rewards him with whoops of approval.

Cultural anthropology is the study of cultures throughout the world in all their variety. The anthropologist, however, is interested in more than describing quaint customs; he wants to uncover the meaning behind them. How does a particular custom help a people adjust to the demands of its physical and social environment? What is the significance, for example, of a parent's goading his four-year-old into striking him? Does it have anything to do with the fact that the Yanomamö must bring up tough, ferocious warriors if they are to survive their frequent feuding with their neighbors?

Not content with what he sees on the surface, the anthropologist is always asking questions: Why are husbands in some societies permitted more than one wife? Why is it incestuous among some peoples for even the most distant relatives to marry? Why, as in America, do families change their place of residence so frequently? Why are initiation rites so severe for boys and so gentle for girls in many places? The anthropologist is not merely curious. He wants to find the contribution that each custom makes to the maintenance of a culture.

A culture is more than a hodgepodge of customs and habits that a people somehow or other managed to put together over the centuries. It is a unified structure in which the various parts mesh to make up a fairly consistent social organization. At first sight a strange practice may seem foolish or incomprehensible. But when seen as part of the life of the people who use it and in terms of its contribution to the welfare of the community, it may be as sensible and meaningful as any custom to which we are accustomed.

When we first hear about the customs of non-Western peoples we are tempted to think, How queer can you get? The anthropologist, however, does not judge cultures. He does not assign grades of good, bad, or just passing. He appreciates the richness of human behavior among the naked Arunta hunters and gatherers of the northern Australian desert as well as among his students and colleagues at the university. Our particular culture is only one alternative among the many designs for living found on this planet. No people holds the franchise on the right way of being human. "Other fields, other grasshoppers," the Javanese say.

> I do not find it surprising that the blacks paint the devil sparkling white and their gods as black as coal or that certain tribes have a Venus with her breasts hanging down to her thighs, or in brief that all the idolatrous people represent their gods with human faces, and endow them with all their own impulses. It has been well said that if triangles had a god, they would give him three sides.
>
> —*Montesquieu, 1721*

Anthropology once evoked images of bearded adventurers in khaki shorts, gun and camera in hand, barging in on native settlements in the Congo, Polynesia, or the Arctic to investigate the ways of preliterate people. Today, without abandoning research in remote communities, anthropologists are also studying their own societies. Turning in their field work to nightclub patrons, hospital patients, churchgoers, high school students, ghetto dwellers, or supermarket customers, anthropologists are examining the culture of industrial societies with the scientific objectivity they have been trained to use in their study of tribal life.

No culture stands still. In tribal or industrial lands change constantly occurs. Under increasing contact with Western ideas, trade, and industrialization, ways of life that were preva-

More than 2 million people live like these nomads in Somalia, East Africa. Wanderers, they spend much of their lives following their herds in search of forage.

lent in many simple societies just thirty, twenty, or even ten years ago have vanished. Few Arunta still hunt kangaroo. Few Eskimos still build igloos. Headhunters in the Amazon Valley no longer shrink heads—except for the tourist trade. Only for convenience do we continue to use the present tense in this book to describe events in the tribal world of the last half-century.

The life ways of Western societies are also changing so rapidly that each of us can become his own anthropologist. Within a few short years we have witnessed cultural innovations close to home ranging from new styles in clothing, hair, and speech to changes in the status of women, relations within the family, the sexual revolution, the arrival of new religions, and the rise and fall of the youth movement. By the time the prophet looks up from his crystal ball, he may be talking about the past.

Life Styles is as much about ourselves as it is about villagers in the wild Mato Grosso of Brazil or Pueblo Indians in the Southwest American desert. Intended for the beginner in anthropology, it omits such topics as technology, linguistics, and archaeology in favor of the more personal issues of sexual behavior, family relations, puberty, and religion.

To become aware of our own culture is difficult because we have always lived right in its very midst. We take it for granted, as fish accept the water in which they swim. It's far easier to perceive a culture other than our own because the differences startle us. Someone once said that by the end of the first week the new postman on the street becomes invisible. An introduction to alternative ways of living may help us become aware of our own culture with a renewed sense of surprise and appreciation. We may be able to see the postman again.

From the moment he is born a child begins to acquire the culture of his people. Biologically, all children are born in the same way; socially, different peoples have evolved different responses to the arrival of a child in the world. We begin with the birth of the child.

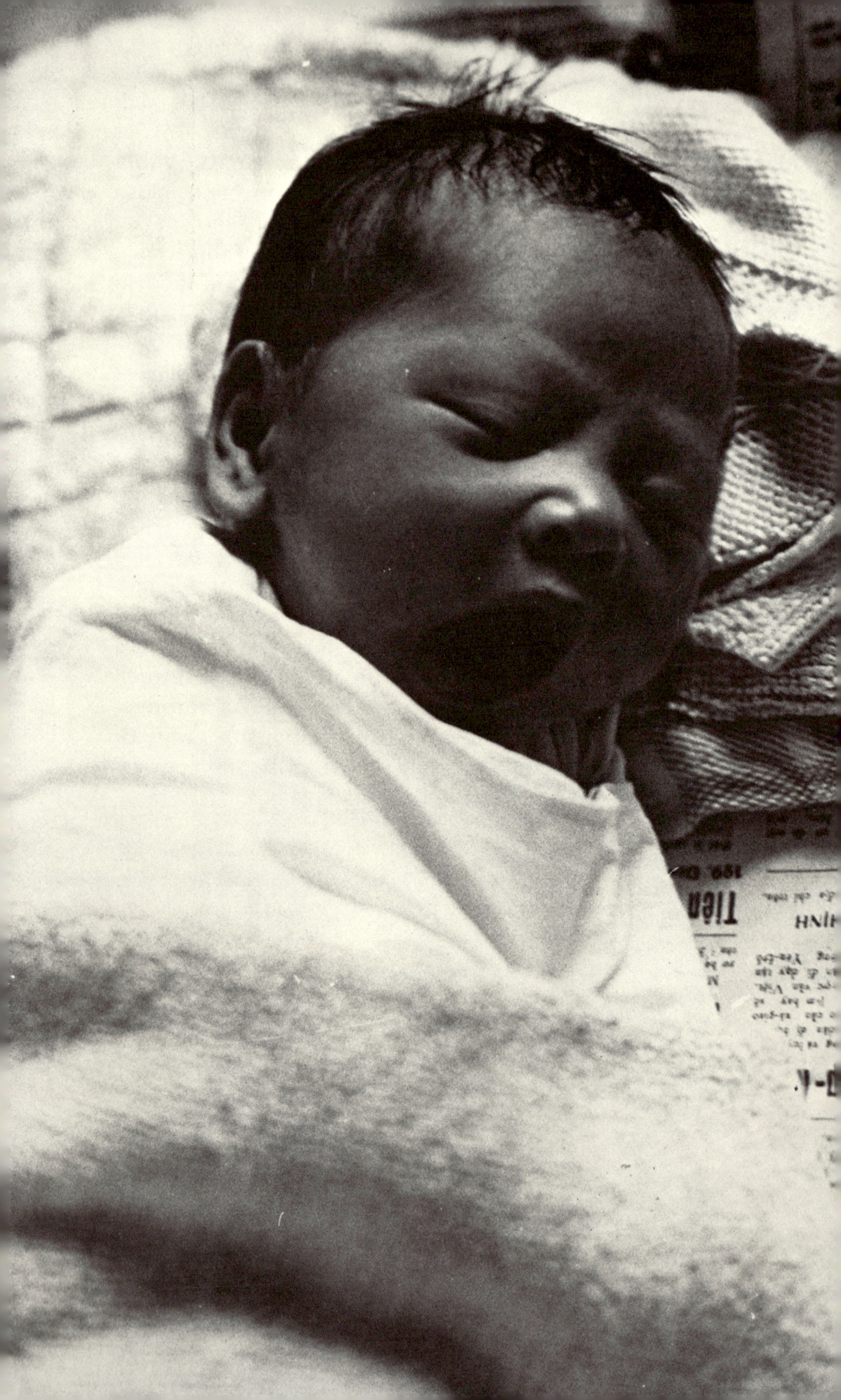

the birth of a child

1

"My Moccasins Need Repair"

SEVEN thousand feet above sea level in the Nilgiri Hills of southern India a bird shrilly announces the coming of dawn. In the dim light an old man kneels before the open door of the village temple and gently whispers to the infant cradled in his arms: "See the temple and the sacred objects within." He rises and, turning toward the glowing east, intones: "See the sky, see the birds, see the trees." Then he slyly adds, "See my moustache." The members of the child's family, surrounding him, softly laugh. The old man carefully lowers the baby to the ground and holds him at the feet of one of his mother's relatives as he again chants: "See the temple, see the sky, see the birds, see the trees." And with this simple ceremony the infant takes his place as a human being among the Toda, a tribal people of India. It is his introduction to the world.

On the other side of the globe, the Hopi Indians of the southwestern American desert isolate the newborn child and his mother in a darkened room for twenty days, during which time he is said to be traveling the path that leads from the underworld to the world of light and people. Before dawn on the twentieth day, the child's paternal grandmother enters the room accompanied by her daughters dressed in long white ceremonial gowns. She washes the child's head, rubs his body with sacred cornmeal, and gives him his name. Keeping watch from a nearby rooftop, the child's father calls out that the sun is about to rise. Strapped to a cradle board the child is carried out of doors by his grandmother who, as the light comes up over the rim of the desert, formally presents him to the sun. Exposed at last to the light, the child may now begin his life on earth.

Social Birth All around the world—in simple as well as in technologically advanced societies—the birth of a child is usually associated with a presentation or ceremony. Biological birth is not enough. A child must be born socially as well. In a sense every child must be born twice.

In societies that possess no written records, public proclamations of birth are especially vital. They announce to the community not only the arrival of a new member but also the creation of new responsibilities for a number of people who now assume such positions as parent, grandparent, godparent, sibling, uncle, or aunt.

Ho, ye sun, moon, stars,
All ye that move in the heavens
I bid you, hear me.
Into your midst
has come a new life.
Consent ye, consent ye,
I implore.
Make its path smooth
That it may travel beyond
the four hills.

—*An Omaha Indian medicine man's introduction of a child to the world*

Laurie and George Guilfoyle
are happy to announce
the birth of their daughter
Jennifer March
Weight: 6 lbs., 10 oz.
May 16, 1971

—*Contemporary American birth announcement*

In America within a few days of the birth of a child a name is selected, announcements are dispatched, a birth certificate is filed. A grinning father distributes cigars and accepts congratulations. Laden with gifts and good wishes, relatives arrive. A christening or circumcision rite soon follows, signaling the child's admission into his family religion. In some societies, however, the public presentation may be delayed for weeks or even months. The Toda ceremony does not take place until three months after the birth of the child. The Hopi do not acknowledge the social existence of the child until almost three weeks have gone by. Why should not all parents rush to broadcast the good news to the world?

> Ah, ah, ah, why have you done this to me, child?
> You chose me as your mother.
> I tried to do everything for you.
> Look at your toys:
> All the things I made for you.
> Why did you desert me, child?
> Please do not stay away.
> Have mercy on me who am your mother,
> Child.
>
> —*Kwakiutl Indian mother's lament for her dead infant*

In a society that lacks the resources of modern medicine, infant mortality can be very high. Parents require no trained demographer to tell them that many infants will not survive the first days of life. The Swazi people of southern Africa refer to a newborn child as a "thing." Only after it has lived for three months does it "become" a person, receive a name, and hear a lullaby sung by its mother for the very first time.

Parents often turn to magic to protect their newborn child against illness and death. The Omaha Indians of the western Plains of America cut a hole in the moccasins of the infant so that should the messenger of death arrive, the child could say to him, "I am not yet ready to journey back to the spirit world; my moccasins need repair." Fearful of black magic, parents in some cultures refuse to give their child a name until he has outlived the perilous years of babyhood. Who knows what harm a sorcerer could commit supplied with the identity of the child?

Should an infant die, parents in some societies try to relieve their grief by pretending that theirs was no child at all. The Ashanti of West Africa used to say that an infant who died was only a ghost pawned off on the parents in place of a real child. Accordingly, instead of being given a proper burial, the corpse was unceremoniously tossed on a rubbish heap. Where infant mortality is high, parents attempt to place an emotional distance between themselves and their newborn, thereby avoiding suffering that would otherwise be unbearable.

In the rest of the country [Nigeria] the official figures say that 350 to 450 children out of every thousand die before their fifth birthday . . . what astounds foreign doctors is the speed with which death can occur in young bodies weakened by a state of perpetual infection. It is thought that virtually every child is infected with malaria, polio and worms.

—New York Times, *1977*

Reshaping the Infant Around the world parents look at their newborn child and then get busy improving on nature. Not willing to leave him as they find him at birth, they attempt to mold him according to the dictates of their life style. During the first eight days following birth, parents in Haiti frequently pinch the infant's nostrils so that they will grow narrow. The cheeks of the baby are burned slightly to protect him from sorcery.

The Tchikrin Indians of central Brazil insert a narrow wooden plug in the lower lip of the male infant a few days after birth. As the child grows older the opening in the lip is gradually enlarged, so that by the time he becomes an adult it can hold a saucerlike plate four inches in diameter. Other people reshape the infant's head. In a number of African societies the infant's soft cranium is bound in cloth to produce a peaked or cone-shaped head. During pre-Columbian times the Mayan In-

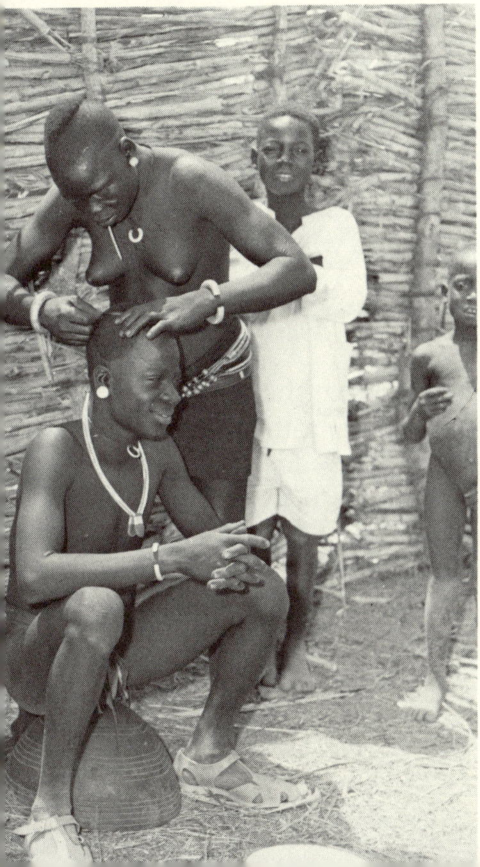

Around the world people turn the human body into a work of art. The change may be permanent, as in flattening the cranium; lengthening the neck; binding the feet; scarring or tattooing the skin; or perforating the earlobes, lips, or nostrils. It may also be temporary, as in the case of hair styling or painting the lips, cheeks, eyelids, or body. • Upper left, the sister of the Sultan of Ruanda-Urandi in central Africa. Right, a Jur woman of the southern Sudan. Lower left, a Kamberi family of northern Nigeria.

dians of Guatemala and Yucatan bound two boards around the head of the newborn child so that the head was pressed into what was considered the ideal human shape. And since crossed eyes were much admired in their society, they also attempted to cross the eyes of the infant by dangling small beads over its nose. In the United States today the circumcision of male infants—the partial removal of the prepuce, or the fold of skin covering the head of the penis—is standard procedure in many maternity hospitals, apparently for hygienic reasons.

The reasons people give for the same custom may differ from community to community. Swaddling, for example, is the practice of keeping the infant tightly bound in strips of cloth. Eastern European Jews said they kept the infant swaddled to ensure that its legs would grow straight. Russians claimed they swaddled because an unrestrained child might harm itself. Polish mothers worried about the infant's fragility if it were not bound. The Pathans in Pakistan were convinced that swaddling comforted the baby.

Fathers and mothers everywhere offer a variety of reasons for altering their infant such as embellishing its appearance, protecting its life, or forestalling illness. Behind each explanation lies the overriding desire to fit the child to the norms of the culture. In a flathead society, a roundhead would be a deviate. Practices that may strike the outsider as foolish or dangerous reassure parents that their child will conform to acceptable models. Custom soothes anxiety.

The Seclusion of Parents In America at the time of birth the infant takes the center of the stage. The mother assumes a secondary role and the father a very minor part. In some tribal societies, however, the parents, and not the child, receive the most attention and care. Who knows but that the supernatural dangers that surround a newborn child will spread to its parents. To protect themselves the parents must therefore engage in prescribed ceremonials, take special medicines, and follow certain diets. Sometimes they must go into seclusion and avoid contact with kin, friends, and neighbors.

Among those who seclude the parents of newborn children are the Indian tribes who live along the Xingu River in the Mato Grosso in the heart of Brazil. The Xinguanos live in huge one-room houses capable of holding five or more families. When their first child is born, the parents retire behind a palm-wood partition they have built around their living area to cut themselves off from the other families in the house. The mother remains behind the barrier for three months and the father for as many as nine months more. To avoid being seen while they are in seclusion, the parents emerge from their hideaway only after dark, flitting about the village like ghosts.

The Xinguanos say that seclusion contributes to the health and safety of baby and parents by defending all of them from the supernatural perils attendant on a child's first year. But why should the father require a far more extended period of retirement than the mother? We who give less credence to the supernatural than the Indians might guess that the custom represents an exaggerated assertion of fatherhood, a pointed reminder to the community that the father, who can so easily be overlooked when a child is born, is also responsible for its coming into the world. And we may also note that seclusion, by relieving parents of social duties, allows them to devote themselves entirely to the care and training of their young baby, an extended maternity-paternity leave many American parents would undoubtedly welcome.

Couvade Xinguano paternal seclusion is a form of *couvade* (French: *couver,* to brood or incubate), the strange custom, at least from our point of view, in which the father behaves as though he were the mother—taking to bed when his wife gives birth, imitating her labor pains, or staying in seclusion after the child is born. Practiced in a number of societies as widely separated as northern Japan, southern India, New Guinea, and South America, couvade appears to be a spectacular demonstration of male parenthood. It certainly associates the father with the newborn child.

Among the mountain Arapesh of New Guinea the father at the time of delivery brings his little wooden pillow and lies down by his wife's side. He is said to be having a baby. Following the birth he remains in strict seclusion with his wife for five days, observing certain taboos* such as touching food only with an implement and scratching himself only with a stick. After the fifth day he is conducted outside and his head is anointed with white paint, a sign that he has borne a child. The father continues to sleep with the mother and child while strictly avoiding sexual relations, for the Arapesh believe that parental sex is harmful to an infant during its first year of life.

Westerners are fascinated by a custom in which a man imitates a woman in labor. What may be of greater significance, however, are some of the taboos a couvadist must follow. The Arapesh avoidance of sexual intercourse, for example, allows a mother at least a year to care for her child without the burden of another pregnancy. In effect, the taboo is a method of birth control.

Although there is little chance that American fathers will ever become couvadists, many of them in recent years have taken on nurturant or mothering tasks once considered the sole responsibility of women. Formerly barred from the hospital delivery room, husbands now are frequently encouraged to be present during the birth of their child not only to help their wives during labor but also to share in the experience. At home young husbands prepare formulas, change diapers, and get up during the night when the baby cries. With the nursing bottle, one of the great inventions of Western technology, they can assume the nurturing function, once confined to lactating females, of feeding the baby. In several states public agencies grant male employees *paternity* leaves of absence to take care

*A taboo is the prohibition of an act, the violation of which brings an automatic and supernatural punishment.

In some tribal societies fathers may take on child-care tasks that would have been considered the responsibility of the mother in the United States—at least until recently. • Father and child in a village near Goroka in New Guinea.

of young children at home—while their wives go out to work. Although only women can give birth to children, males can mother them.

"My father would not have lifted a finger to make dinner or change a diaper," said Mr. Terranova, who works in the family's bakery supply business in the Bronx and sometimes cooks dinner for his children. "In the old days that just wasn't the manly thing. The important thing back then was bringing home money. Now you got to give of yourself, too."

—New York Times, *1976*

Rites of Passage Will a baby live? Will he be normal? How will he grow up? The arrival of a child in any society is a time of wondering, of high hopes, and of deep anxiety.

When God birthed you, you were sweet and dear. But before He could turn around He sees that a bum has growed up. Even He doesn't know how it happened.

—A fourth-grader, Harlem, New York, 1976

Around the world parents try to control the natural and supernatural forces that may help or hurt their newborn. Some withdraw behind quiet seclusion barriers; others throw a big bash. Priests sprinkle holy water; medicine men invoke the support of the spirits. Well-wishers send silver spoons, surgeons improve on nature, fathers reassert their claim to parenthood. Customs surrounding the birth of a child may vary widely in different societies, but behind many of them we may discern the overwhelming desire of parents to guide their child through the perils of an uncertain biological process into life and sound health.

Anthropologists call the ceremonies attendant on a child's entrance into the world *rites of passage*. Marking a person's passage in life from one social stage to another, rites of passage are celebrated not only at the time of birth but on other critical occasions such as marriage, retirement, or death. Life may be continuous, but all societies set up ceremonial mileposts along the way to ease the transition into adulthood, marriage, or old age. Baptisms, confirmations and bar mitzvahs, betrothals, weddings, retirement dinners, and funeral services are all rites of passage.

Rites of passage help people accept their new responsibilities and at the same time remind the community to treat them in a manner appropriate to their new positions in life. The ceremonies associated with birth alert parents and relatives to their new duties. Marriage rites announce the formation of a network of new relationships and obligations among people who were formerly strangers. Death rites help knit together the emotion-torn lives of the survivors. Of all the rites of passage in simple societies, the best known are those that help young people establish their bearings as they emerge out of childhood and enter into young adulthood.

We turn to the time in the life of young people in tribal groups when they put aside their childhood status and take up the privileges and responsibilities of maturity.

puberty rites

2

"A Boy Must Come Out from Under His Mother's Skirts"

A GIRL wakes one morning and discovers that she is menstruating for the first time. In America the occasion would arouse no public interest and the girl would continue to live as though she were still a child. In many tribal societies, however, the onset of puberty (Latin: *pubertas,* adulthood), or the beginning of sexual maturity, is an event demanding public recognition and, frequently, a celebration. A Cheyenne Indian father, learning that his daughter had experienced her first menses, shouted the good news to all his neighbors and gave away a fine horse.

Navajo Debut Today among the Navajo Indians of the southwestern United States the occasion of a girl's first menstruation is marked by an elaborate four-day ceremony called the *kinaalda.* In preparation for the festivities the girl is kept home from school and put to work doing household chores and grinding the corn for an immense six-foot-long cake. Each morning an older relative brushes the girl's hair to give it beauty and massages her body to assure that she will grow straight. At sundown on the fourth day, dressed in traditional Navajo costume and laden with all the jewelry her family can borrow on short notice, the girl takes her place in the family lodge surrounded by a circle of one hundred or more guests. Singing led by a medicine man begins and continues all through the night. To keep the girl from falling asleep, someone is appointed to prod her every time she nods.

At dawn, her hair having been washed, the girl runs as far as she can toward the sacred east, her wet tresses streaming after her, followed by a whooping crowd of young relatives. On her return she cuts the cake and passes it to the guests together with oranges, watermelon, and candy. By eight in the morning the ceremony comes to an end, the guests depart, and the young lady can at last take her rest.

The Navajo *kinaalda* is a crash course in homemaking and an announcement that a girl is eligible for marriage. A few short days ago she was a little girl romping with her friends in the schoolyard. Now she has become a young woman upon whom suitors may call. Although no more than twelve or thirteen she must give up the ways of childhood and assume the duties and privileges of womanhood. All her life she will think back fondly to her *kinaalda.* She has made her debut.

The Boy Hermits In every human society there comes a time when young people must leave childhood and enter the adult world. Unwilling to leave the outcome to individual decision or physical maturation, each culture sets up ground rules for the transition.

Among the Xinguano tribes, seclusion is used not only to see parents through the critical period following childbirth but also to transform young people into grown-ups. At the age of nine or ten a Xinguano boy gives up his playmates and goes into seclusion behind a barrier in one corner of his house. There he lives by himself for several years and is seen only by close kin. His mother brings him food and water, and his father instructs him in adult skills. From time to time his father administers a number of magic potions to turn the boy into a good fisherman and hunter and scarifies his body with a fish-tooth scraper to make him strong and healthy. When not taking lessons or practicing handicrafts by himself, the boy is supposed to concentrate his thoughts on wrestling. Xinguano boys dream about becoming champion wrestlers the way American youths fantasize about playing for the Dallas Cowboys or the Cincinnati Reds.

Actually, time passes slowly behind the darkened barrier, so that after the first year or so the boy spends much of his day staring out at village life through a hole he has poked in the house wall. About the time that he reaches puberty he takes to wandering outside his house at night and in short order becomes involved in affairs with girls. As soon as his father learns of these extracurricular activities, he tears down the barrier and unceremoniously evicts his son. No longer a little boy, the youth will shortly assume an adult role as a fisherman, hunter, farmer, and head of his own family.

Across the Pacific among the Tchambuli mountain people of New Guinea the passage from childhood to adulthood begins between the ages of eight and twelve when a boy is scarified with designs scratched into his back. He leaves his family and goes to live in the men's clubhouse, coming out only at night disguised in a long rain cape, his body covered with white clay. After several months he emerges into the light of day. His body is washed and he is presented with a woven belt, a bamboo gourd, and shell ornaments—gifts that signify his graduation from childhood.

Ceremonies such as the Navajo *kinaalda* or the seclusion of young boys among the Tchambuli and Xinguanos are rites of passage that mark the transition from childhood to adulthood. Since they often occur about the time of the onset of sexual maturity, they are also known as puberty rites. The mere fact that a young person is growing up physically is not enough to confer adult status; there must be some social acknowledgment such as a celebration, a religious ceremony, a withdrawal followed by a return to the community, or, perhaps, the accomplishment of an adult task. Among the cannibal Asmat of New Guinea a youth was not deemed a man until he had killed an enemy, beheaded him, prepared a pudding of his brains mixed with sago palm, and eaten it.

A young Crow Indian went into the wilderness by himself in search of a vision that would bring him supernatural power. To bring on the vision he would starve and torture himself, sometimes cutting off part of a finger and offering it as a sacrifice to the morning star with this prayer:

> I give you this finger joint.
> In return give me a good horse,
> A good wife and a tent of my own.

In the midst of his torment a mysterious stranger, a dwarf, or a wild animal would appear and give the youth a magical song or gift to protect him from harm. Emerging from the wilderness, the young man returned as one ready to assume the duties and rights of an adult.

All societies do not require a formal rite of passage to cross the threshold into adulthood. While some celebrate the occasion with pomp and circumstance, others barely give it passing notice. On the islands of Polynesia in the western Pacific a boy beginning to sprout facial and pubic hair simply left the company of the women by whom he had been raised and began to eat in the men's house. A Tchikrin Indian boy who reaches puberty simply adopts two symbols of manhood: he covers his penis with a penis sheath and replaces the child-sized plug in his lower lip with a saucer-sized plate. And, lo, he is a man.

When a child does a man's work, he is a man.

—*Papago Indian saying*

In some societies young people move into adulthood through the institution of the age set, which is a group of people of the same sex and similar age who go through the stages of life together. Among the Nyakyusa of Lake Nyasa in southeastern Africa boys stay at home with their parents until they are about twelve years of age. Then they go off together to live in their own boys' village, where they take charge of their own community affairs and responsibilities. When they reach the age of twenty-five the young men marry and bring their wives into their village. After another ten years have gone by, the fathers of the young men retire from public office and turn all political authority over to them.

Death and Resurrection Whether public or private, puberty rites are often arranged like a three-act play. In Act I a child vanishes. In Act II he lives apart from his home and relatives. During this period his hair style or clothing may be changed; his body mutilated, scarified, or tatooed. He may receive instruction in adult skills and listen to lectures from the elders about his future conduct and the traditions of his people. In Act III he returns, his appearance and personality altered, no longer a child. It is as though he had died, been buried, and then miraculously reborn as a new person. Among some peoples the drama is carried so far that the returning young person behaves as though he were a newborn child who must learn to eat, to stand, and to recognize his parents and friends. Often the final curtain includes a ceremony in which the youth is reintegrated into community life.

Puberty Rites Can Hurt In the tribal world puberty ceremonies are usually far more impressive and more painful for boys than for girls. One phase of the puberty rites of the Arunta, a hunting and gathering people of northern Australia, began with a tossing ritual in which the men threw the boys high into the air and then beat them as they hit the ground. The beating, the Arunta claimed, taught the boys to respect their elders; the tossing encouraged the boys to grow tall.

Afterwards, each boy was conducted to a hideaway in the

wilderness where he lived by himself, lighting his own fire and gathering his own food. Following several days of solitary living the boys were assembled to be circumcised, receive new names, and hear lectures devoted to good conduct and morality.* But the ordeal was not over. Six weeks later, their wounds barely healed, the boys submitted to subincision, a radical operation in which the underside of the penis is slit to the urethra. Then followed a great festival at which guests from other tribes, parents, and kinfolk danced and feasted for as many days as the food lasted. The festivities ended with the presentation to each boy of a bull roarer, a flat wooden board with notched edges which makes a roaring sound when whirled on a string. Said to inspire both fear and passion in women, it was a kind of diploma which bestowed upon the initiated the rights of full-fledged adult members in their society.

Across the Indian Ocean in Southeast Africa, boys of the Thonga tribe were prepared for manhood by attending a "circumcision" school whose curriculum included circumcision, ingestion of vile foods, exposure to cold, and other forms of humiliation and hazing. On the occasion of his circumcision a boy ran the gauntlet between men armed with clubs. His clothing was stripped from him, his hair was cut, and he was set against a rock facing a man covered with a lion's mane. He was struck from behind and as he turned to see who had hit him, the lion man leaped forward and cut off his foreskin. Afterwards, he was secluded for three months before being allowed to return home.†

Why should puberty rites sometimes seem to resemble the scenario of a horror show? One possible explanation is that

*Why is circumcision, the removal of the foreskin of the penis, so widespread a puberty rite? It has been thought that since the penis is associated with the adult male role, the circumcision becomes a permanent marker indicating the new position of a youth in his society, or, as we would say, separating the men from the boys. The knife sharpens the lesson.

†By no means are all male initiation rites so severe. In a sample of fifty-five societies only eighteen had features as dramatic as the Arunta or Thonga.

harsh rites are closely related to the severity of the demands that are made on the adults of a society. The Plains Indian youth who mutilated himself to induce a vision was also hardening himself to withstand torture if he were captured by an enemy in time of war.

This explanation apparently makes sense when we consider that girls usually escape the rigors of male puberty rites. A girl may have her hair style changed, her ears pierced, or her teeth blackened, but cruelty and mutilation are unusual. The most arduous task of the Navajo girl was staying up all night. Generally a girl receives instructions in matters relating to sex, childbirth, contraception, marriage, and household skills—the ritual period ending with a public feast at which she wears grown-up clothes and a woman's hairdo for the first time.

In central Africa among tribal people who prized an ample female form, girls were secluded in "fatting" houses until they achieved the desired plumpness. In the Andaman Islands in the Indian Ocean a girl was hidden in a hut where, adorned with leaves, she sat for several days with her legs under her and her arms folded, fed as though she were a baby. Renamed for a tree currently in bloom, she became a flower ready for fertilization and the children she would soon bear. In British Columbia Indian girls dropped pebbles down their dresses so that their children would come into the world as easily as the stones slid to the ground.

The different treatment of boys and girls seems to foreshadow what will be expected of them as men and women. Girls are prepared for homemaking and childbearing, boys for hunting, fighting, and other male pursuits. Are rites of passage, then, forms of vocational guidance?

"A Boy Must Come Out From Under His Mother's Skirts" Still a word of caution is in order. We want to be wary of explanations that *cross over* from culture to culture. Tribal peoples—no less than peoples in large-scale industrial societies—are not rubber stamps of each other. Customs that look

In tribal and peasant societies a young person must put aside childish things and take up the duties of adulthood at an early age. Amanatou, a seventeen-year-old girl in northern Cameroon, West Africa, does the family laundry, watches her young brothers and sisters, and after supper leads them in reciting the Koran. Eldest of the unmarried twenty-two children in the household, Amanatou also attends a Western-type school six days a week in order to prepare for social work.

alike to the outside observer may have different functions in different communities.

One theory concerning puberty rites strongly suggests that there is a close relationship between sleeping arrangements for young boys and the type of ceremonies found in their subsequent initiation into adult life. Rites are most dramatic where the boys as very young children live closer to their mothers than to their fathers, but when grown up are called upon to engage in activities such as hunting and fighting which demand a very high degree of personal courage and intimate cooperation with the men of the group. Such situations seem to arise in societies in which it is the custom for the young boy to be nursed by his mother for several years after birth and to sleep in the same bed or hammock with her, while the father sleeps in his own separate quarters. Under these circumstances a boy may tend to develop an enduring emotional tie with his mother to the exclusion of his father and other males.

But if the survival of the group depends on the utmost cooperation and solidarity of all the men, how is the boy's attachment to his mother to be broken? How is he to sever his female identification and transfer his emotional allegiance to the males of the band or tribe? A puberty rite, the theory goes, is a crash course in masculinity which propels the boy out of his mother's warm protecting arms into the world of men, work, and fighting. "A boy must come out from under his mother's skirts."

Probably no society has so clearly illustrated the function of male puberty rites in sundering a boy's tie to his home and mother as the Tiwi, a hunting and gathering people of northern Australia. Suddenly one evening while the family is gathered about the fire, four heavily-armed strangers invade the camp. "We have come for your son," they ominously declare. The mother begins to howl. The father rushes to the defense of his son, who in desperate fright clings to his mother. But the strangers tear the boy free and bear him off into the night. Only later does the boy learn that the kidnapping has been staged as part of his initiation into manhood. He has literally been torn from his mother and his childhood, and his allegiance has been shifted from his home and family to the men of the band.

Another and related theory is based on the observation that where the men of the group engage in very few tasks that take them away from the company of their women and children, initiation rites tend to be mild or entirely absent. In societies, however, where the men conduct secret ceremonies hidden from their women or engage in activities from which females are barred, such as warfare, initiation rites are likely to be dramatic. The thought is that where adult males belong to a tight-knit exclusive organization, a highly spectacular ritual is required to identify the young male with his adult group.

Whether or not a particular theory is valid for all communities in which there are dramatic initiations into manhood, puberty rites can only be understood as part of a whole culture. Seen by itself a harsh rite may seem shocking or altogether absurd. Fitted into the needs of a society which demands that the adult males work and fight staunchly together, the custom takes on a measure of sense and utility.

Fraternity and Sorority Rites Can the concept of male solidarity give us a clue to the differences between fraternity and sorority initiation rites in the United States? Though hazing can be very rough on male pledgees—in some cases leading to serious injury or even death—it is quite gentle or even completely absent for female candidates.

Some of our so-called brains don't join but we get a lot of smart girls, cheerleaders, athletes, all kinds of girls. They go through the usual pledging. They have to handle chicken guts and worms. They have to wear ridiculous outfits to school and sing songs and put on skits. . . . It's fun.

—An American high school teacher's description of a sorority initiation, 1974

The nineteen-year-old freshman who suffocated in a grave he had to dig . . . as part of his initiation into a fraternity is at least the fourth student to die as a result of such senseless rites on American campuses. . . .

—New York Times *editorial, 1974*

Aside from the American tradition of treating females more gently than males, is it possible to locate the source of the difference in the advantages of long-term allegiance and cooperation among fraternity members? Sororities tend to loosen their hold on members after graduation from college for a number of reasons, including the pressures of family and household responsibilities. Fraternities, on the other hand, tend to remain tightly knit, exclusive organizations which provide their members with lifelong associations in business, politics, and social life. May we surmise that harsh fraternity rites, despite heavy public criticism, persist at least in part because they help to promote invaluable male solidarity among members? Bearing in mind the dangers of cross-cultural explanations, especially from simple tribal groups to complex industrial states, we can only say that the idea is highly provocative.

Miracle Drama A puberty rite may also be interpreted as a public spectacle in which a child is magically transformed into an adult. Frightening, amusing, exciting, with swift changes in scene, pace, costume, and makeup, the play is a miracle drama which receives the rapt attention of the entire community, especially of the young person who is called upon to play many of the parts, first as little helpless victim and finally as victor, hero, and grown-up.

A puberty ceremony is also a solemn proclamation to all the community that a young person's status, his position in society, has been changed. Duly admitted to the company of grown men and women, he cannot fail their expectations. Initiates are not likely to act like children again. The Navajo girl will never again play in the schoolyard with the other children. The Arunta boy will never again tag after his mother. There are few backsliders. Despite the fear and distress they may have experienced, people in tribal societies often look back with pride and affection to the time when they made their passage into the world of men and women.

Puberty, like birth, is a biological fact common to all human societies; yet it is socially acknowledged in a wide variety of ways. What happens to young people in contemporary Western states after they become pubescent?

adolescence in america

3

"You Have to Make It to Get What You Want"

ON A sunny afternoon at a busy intersection in a large eastern city Jonathan Miller, aged eighteen, wearing a sunbonnet and a long Victorian-style gown, his face painted in grotesque colors, stands at the curb, a striped umbrella over his head. Toward evening a group of young men appear and hurry him to a house where they compel him to eat evil-tasting food, do exhausting pushups, and submit to other humiliating and cruel acts. But then at midnight they suddenly end the ordeal and welcome Jonathan into their fellowship. They show him the sacred books and relics of their order, reveal their secret handgrip and password, and finally slip a ring embossed with Greek letters on his finger. Jonathan has been initiated into an American college fraternity.

What Is Adolescence? Each year all over the United States high school and college students gain admission to fraternities and sororities by participating in elaborate rituals that resemble tribal puberty rites. Jonathan, for example, was separated from friends and family; he was subjected to severe hazing; finally, he was restored to his society bearing a new status, that of fraternity brother. Still the similarity is only superificial. A puberty ceremony is a true rite of passage which conveys the initiate into a basically new position in life. Jonathan may now be a fraternity brother, but his fundamental status in society has not changed. He belongs as he did before his initiation to a transitional category of young Americans who are neither adults nor children but are designated by such terms as *adolescent, teenager, youth,* or *young person.*

Over 20 percent of the American people fall into this category, and their numbers are rapidly increasing. By 1980 out of a population of 220 million, 45 million will range in age from fourteen to twenty-four. At the present time the majority of Americans are under the age of twenty-one. Only at the foundation of the Republic was so large a proportion of the population so young.

Yet despite their numbers, the culture has great difficulty in defining just who these young people are. Who is an adolescent? Who is a youth? Biologically, adolescence is the period that extends from the onset of puberty to the attainment of full reproductive capacity. The average age at which American females experience their first menstrual flow is 12.8 years. Few girls, however, are capable of childbearing before the age of fifteen. Boys display outward signs of puberty about the fourteenth year, but most do not secrete fertile semen before the fifteenth. Youth is generally designated as the stage between the attainment of reproductive maturity and the beginning of adulthood.

All very neat, except that no specific age determines just when adulthood begins. The age of twenty-one is only a convenient fiction. If an adult is a person who has come of age, the question remains, "At what age?" American society bestows adult status not in one single package but in a number of little parcels delivered at different times. There is an age for getting into bars or X-rated movies, an age for sexual consent, an age for leaving school, an age for operating a short-wave transmitter or a motorcycle, an age for getting married, an age for obtaining a hunting license, an age for voting or running for the city council. The ages vary from state to state and often from county to county. Collecting all the little parcels may take well over a decade.

Some tribal peoples make the transition from childhood to adulthood in a few days or months, with little or no awareness of adolescence and youth as social institutions. A Navajo girl is snatched out of the playground and four days later is catapulted into womanhood. Among the Karimojong, a herding people of Uganda in East Africa, a boy has his head shaved about the time of puberty. As soon as his hair grows back it is plastered down with mud and tied with a chain, a symbol that he is now a man who may marry and raise a family of his own.

The recognition of adolescence and youth as transitional stages between childhood and adulthood is a recent development in Western society. In Europe until the eighteenth century young people had no special status. They dressed as adults, they worked as adults, they were imprisoned and hanged as adults. They loved as adults. Romeo and Juliet were thrust into a tragic romance at an age when most young Americans are completing junior high school. In America before the twentieth century adolescence was not commonly recognized as part of the life cycle. Youths as young as Jonathan Miller were in some form of apprenticeship or ran their own businesses and in many cases raised their own families. Only in recent years have adolescence and youth achieved a special place in the lives of young people both in the United States and in other industrialized countries.

Prolonging Childhood Probably no society on earth delays the entrance of young people into the adult world longer than the United States does. Their dependency extends far beyond the time when many are capable of assuming the rights and obligations of mature citizens. Physically fit, sexually potent, and mentally alert, they nevertheless remain subject to restrictions appropriate to small children. At an age when youths in tribal communities are skilled craftspeople, proficient horticulturists, devoted householders, and political and religious leaders, many young Americans are hazing pledgees, tossing Frisbees, cramming for examinations, or daydreaming about

Over the last century the age of the onset of puberty has dropped precipitously. In 1840 the average young female in Europe or America had her first menses at seventeen. Today her counterpart starts to menstruate at about twelve. Probably as a result of improved medical care and nutrition, adolescents in industrial countries throughout the world are becoming sexually mature at an earlier age than ever before. • Young adolescents in Switzerland.

what they will someday be. Even after graduation from school a few of them, uncertain of their social identity and fearful of the mysterious perils of maturity, linger in a never-never land where they adopt the manners, fashions, speech, and causes of their juniors. Youth becomes an addiction on which they are hooked, long past the age their contemporaries are earning their own living and raising their own families.

Most young people of the middle class, although they may chafe at the restrictions imposed because of their age, learn to accept a status that permits them to devote themselves to their studies. Since a college diploma no longer guarantees a job, some young people go on to graduate school and then to post-graduate education. The graduate student was once defined as a person who did not know enough to go home when the party was over. Today, however, because of the insatiable demand of the economy for ever higher levels of technical competency, the doors to many careers will not open without graduate training. On many campuses serious hardworking students in their late twenties and even thirties, some with their own families, are still dependent on the support of their parents. They have yet to achieve full adult status.

Growing Up Absurd From the point of view of an outside observer young people in America—at least those of the middle class—are growing up under ideal conditions. They have more material possessions than any past youth generation. Unburdened by the need to earn their own living, they may prepare for any number of careers. Outside of class they can play at games on campuses that often resemble country clubs. In a sexually permissive time they may have affairs without fear of administrative disapproval. Apparently, they have it made.

Yet no generation of young people has been assailed with so many problems. Close to 40 percent of entering high school students drop out before graduation. Many who remain in school complain of boredom, apathy, and lack of relevance in their studies. Juvenile delinquency both within the inner city and in the suburbs is growing rapidly. Venereal disease rates among youth are soaring. Millions of teen-agers drink to excess. Suicide is the second major cause of death among young Americans.*

*The first cause of adolescent death is automobile accidents. Because suicide is underreported, a substantial number of listed deaths by accident may also be suicide.

Well, the people I hung around with were big acid heads. One day a friend asked if I wanted to get stoned and I said yes.

—*A twelve-year-old American drug addict*

Each year more than one million young people run away from home. Most return after a few days, but some are never heard from again. Calls from runaways and their parents pour into the switchboards of the two national tollfree telephone exchanges for runaways at the rate of more than a thousand a month. Some of these young people aimlessly wander strange city streets, asking passersby for spare change. Others stand on the side of highways dressed in jeans and T-shirts, sleeping bags on their backs, holding a cardboard sign that may read *New York, San Francisco, Boston,* or *New Orleans*—anywhere but home! A number of films and novels in recent years have portrayed young people on the road on a motorcycle, in a bus, or on foot, going nowhere in particular, their destination uncertain. Marginal persons, rootless, discontented, and alienated, these youths are "growing up absurd."

Kids are like new wine. They have no function but to age.

—*Robert Petersen, National Institute of Mental Health*

Coming of Age in Samoa Older Americans may be distressed by the behavior of young people, but they are probably not surprised. Adults expect adolescence to be a time of turmoil. Young people are supposed to undergo emotional crises, to feel passionately about events and ideas. Brimful of fresh energy, adolescents are not expected to be conforming, well mannered, or obedient. Given all the physiological changes brought about by puberty, isn't it only natural that young people should be restless and troublesome? Adolescence can never be a quiet trip.

But, in fact, are the disturbances of young persons a *natural* part of growing up? Or are they primarily a response to the pressures built into the life style of particular societies? Are there cultures in which adolescence can be a quiet trip?

Fifty years ago the American anthropologist Margaret Mead went to Samoa in the South Pacific to determine how Polynesian girls responded to adolescence. The passage from childhood to maturity, she discovered, was quite casual. At ten or eleven, girls gave up their little playmates and began to wear grown-up clothing. Unlike most young females in America—who at least until the 1950s deferred first intercourse until their early or middle twenties—Samoan girls at puberty entered into a number of sexual affairs, one of which eventually ended in marriage.

On the basis of her Samoan observations Margaret Mead theorized that Western beliefs about the universality of adolescent problems were open to serious doubt.* Since growing up could be marked by perpetual crisis in one society and by enduring calm in another, whatever disturbed Western youth was caused not so much by the biological changes of puberty as by the stresses to which the youth were exposed. Mead concluded that the casual nature of adolescence in one society, like the restless nature of adolescence in another, was linked to the way young people were treated by their culture.

Future Shock Educational demands on young people in Western countries are far higher than in any pre-industrial society. Skills become more difficult to master as levels of technology rise. Those who seek upper-status careers must be prepared to accept years of academic struggle. Almost nowhere is the spirit of competition more intense than in the colleges. And as women are admitted to programs formerly dominated by males the struggle grows even more keen. The nightmare race for grades had not fallen on Samoa when Margaret Mead did her field work there.

* Several anthropologists have suggested that the absence of unrest among Samoan teen-agers was the result of apathy or indifference brought on by the collapse of the old native way of life following the arrival of the Europeans.

To the pressures of the present we may add uncertainties about the future. Youth unrest seems to be most evident when changes in society are most rapid. Since World War II young people have witnessed the exploration of space, the development of nuclear power, the automation of industry, the deterioration of the environment, the decay of great cities, the exposure of corruption in high public office, and the revolution in sexual attitudes and behavior. Science fiction would be hard put to keep up with the transformations in institutions, technology, customs, and values that have taken place in a single generation.

The tempo of change grows ever faster. Changes that once took a century to complete are over and done in less than a decade. The past becomes increasingly remote, the future increasingly immediate. Who can predict what the life of today's young people will be like when they come of age in the closing years of the twentieth century? Their science textbooks often become outdated before they leave school. Their training often becomes obsolescent before they answer their first want ad. The industry for which they expect to work may vanish from town, state, or even the country. Impermanence is the name of the game.

> No one will live all his life in the world into which he was born and no one will die in the world in which he worked in his maturity.
>
> —*Margaret Mead*

In primitive and peasant societies time appears to stand still; the present seems to repeat the past. A young person follows in the path of his parents, and his children follow in his. He confidently faces the tomorrow that will echo today. In industrial societies time is not a comfort but a constant challenge to meet new changes. A young person does not expect to repeat the experiences of his parents but to strike out on his own. Like Alice in Wonderland he must run just to keep from falling behind.

In industrial societies adolescence is a period when young people are in a state of almost constant movement. Whether at home or abroad they are usually on the go. • These young people in France contemplate turning a wreck into a sleek racing car.

Where rival groups, religions, political parties, and social causes compete for his allegiance, the young person is confronted with a dazzling array of choices. He cannot use tradition as his guide. The decisions must be his own, for he will eventually be held responsible for their consequences.

To whom shall young people turn for guidance and reassurance as they journey into the future? In tribal communities the answer is, "To the elders." Where change is minimal it seems natural to follow the advice of parents, grandparents, older relatives, and the village headman. But in a rapidly changing world the bearers of the wisdom of the past must compete for the attention of their children with television personalities, political leaders, teachers, their children's friends, or contempo-

In industrial societies the family has turned over much of the responsibility for the education and guidance of young people to outside institutions. Children take many of their cues for manners, speech, goals, and choice of friends not from parents but from teachers, public figures, agemates, television personalities, and their own youth culture. Whether in Russia or in the United States a far wider range of behavior patterns is available to young people than ever before. • Tanya, a fifteen-year-old Moscow schoolgirl, and her parents do not seem able to communicate.

rary teen-age idols. The rejection of the elders as prophets and heroes would be unthinkable in most small-scale societies.

Becoming an Adult in America One response young people in industrial lands may make to the demands made upon them, as well as to their anxieties about the future, is to cling to the present, embrace freedom from adult responsibility, and sample the goodies as long as the supply holds out—in other words, to prolong childhood as long as possible. Despite this temptation, however, the vast majority know when the party is over. How do these young people arrive at adult status?

Human beings do not merely grow up biologically; they grow up culturally. Each society sets the ground rules for determining how its young people are to be transformed into adults. Tribal communities usually emphasize the rule of *ascription:*

adult status is *ascribed,* or assigned to the young person who has reached a certain age. The community takes a good part of the responsibility and not only stages the rites of passage for transforming him into an adult but also frequently selects his bride, presents him with a job and the tools of his occupation, and ushers him into the civil, military, and religious organizations of the adult society.

In contemporary Western societies, on the other hand, adult status is not so much ascribed as *achieved* or earned. There is little approaching the tribal model in which young people are symbolically divested of their childhood and welcomed into adulthood in ceremonies marked by circumcision, mutilation, seclusion, apparent rebirth, or other emotionally charged rites. A young person is expected to make it on his own. Not by public rite, but by individual decision and effort will he achieve social and economic maturity.

Jonathan Miller will ultimately make up his mind to leave his parents' household and set up a home of his own. He will decide when and whom he will marry; he will select his own occupation and go out and get himself a job. He will seek admission to social clubs, civic organizations, and other adult groups. His attainment of maturity will be primarily a personal achievement. In contrast to young people in many tribal societies, he will be a self-made adult.

You have to study certain things to get a degree and you have to have a degree to make it, and you have to make it to get what you want.

—*An American college student, 1974*

Perhaps at this point we should remind ourselves that we have been talking primarily about middle-class young people. Adolescence comes out differently in different societies. It also comes out differently within the boundaries of a highly complex society such as America. The life of a young person in Appalachia, the Puerto Rican barrio or black ghetto of a great city, or a slum of migratory farm workers in California bears

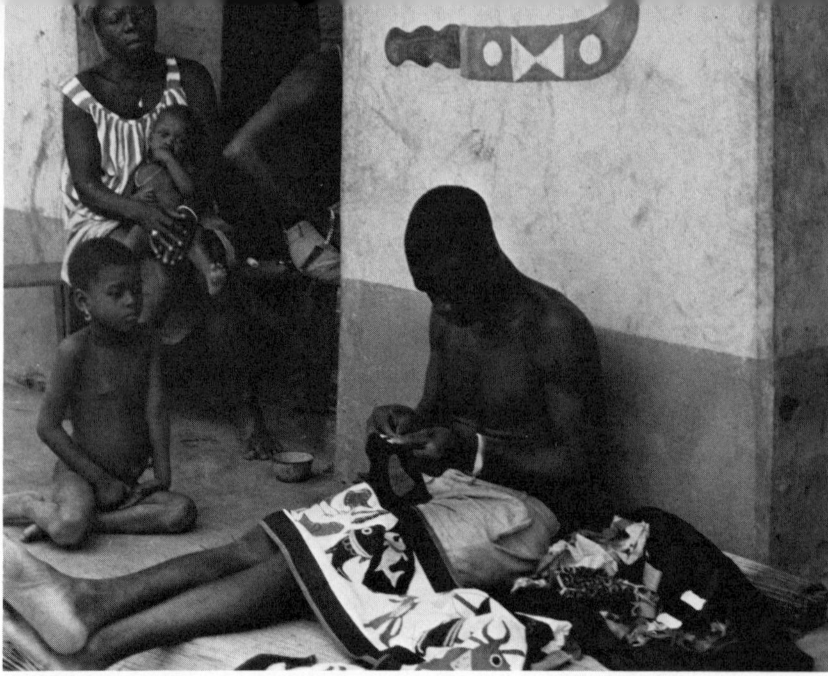

Ascribed statuses are assigned to a person because of inborn characteristics such as race, sex, age, kinship, or inheritance, which the individual can do little to alter or escape. Achieved statuses are earned through individual accomplishment. Such statuses include hunter, runner, storyteller, politician, basket maker, student, teacher, and—like this man in Dahomey, West Africa—tapestry weaver.

little resemblance to that of a middle-class white college student. For the underprivileged, adolescence will be all too short. Schooling will end early. What lies ahead will frequently be a dead-end job, unemployment, or entrance to the relief rolls.

In any society many of our statuses are ascribed; that is they come to us by way of our age, sex, religion, class, family position, and ethnic origin. We have, for example, no part in determining our racial status. Even in a democracy ascribed statuses determine in large measure our social and economic prospects. Unlike Jonathan Miller not all Americans will enjoy full opportunity to make good.

Adolescence as Adaptation Assuming that the adolescent problems of young people are related to the refusal of Western society to allow them the full exercise of their powers, why should we not let our youth like those in small-scale communities assume the rights and privileges of adulthood at an earlier age? As Thoreau said over a century ago: "Students should not play at life or study it merely while the community supports them at this expensive game but earnestly live it. . . . How could youth better learn to live than by at once trying the experiment of living?"

An institution such as adolescence, however, has no independent life of its own which would allow it to be moved freely from culture to culture. Rather is it intimately related to every aspect of living within society. What makes good sense in one community, or in one individual's time, may prove disastrous in another. In the present-day industrial state, the prolongation of adolescence has vital adaptive advantages; that is, it contributes to the welfare of both the individual and the society.

Consider, for example, what would happen if most young people now at school attempted to find adult work! In a small-scale community which relies on simple tools and human muscle power, there is always a job on hand for young people. A small-scale community is usually a full-employment economy. In the industrial state, however, young people would be competing with their parents for scarce jobs. Child labor laws not only protect the young person, they protect an economy which requires fewer workers as mechanization increases.

The extension of adolescence also allows time for the education of the scientists, technicians, bureaucrats, and other highly skilled workers on whom the contemporary Western state relies for its survival. The adult skills the Xinguano youth does not absorb from his father behind the seclusion barrier can be quickly picked up on the job. Jonathan Miller's preparation for a career or profession, however, will require long years of education. We may expect that just as the Xinguano boy will not always keep his mind on his training, so Jonathan will sometimes be distracted from his studies by the football calendar, the freshman smoker, or fraternity rituals.

Adolescence is different in different cultures. Luzia is an underfed fourteen-year-old who lives with her parents and seven brothers in a rural area of Brazil. Unlike teen-agers in industrial lands, who can afford to concern themselves with notions about personal identity or political ideals, young people in under-developed regions must deal with such daily problems as lack of food, decent housing, clothing, and education.

Though adolescence secludes young people in a world of their own which must often seem unreal and childlike, it effectively protects them from adult responsibilities before they are ready to assume them. Young people do not grow up in one piece. A youth may be sexually mature but emotionally and socially immature. An eighteen-year-old may be an intelligent voter but an unfit parent.

In small-scale communities young people who enter marriage and parenthood can expect the close support of a host of relatives. The young couple generally moves close to or into the domicile of the family of the husband or wife. In only 5 percent of the world's societies do young people set up their residences removed from their parents. In our own society young couples usually live apart from their families. Yet they may not be mature enough to maintain their own independent households.

In a society where young people have many choices not only of lifework but also of friends, beliefs, and causes, they need time to consider and weigh. Adolescence provides them with a period of delay before they commit themselves to any decision. In a rapidly changing world, according to the American psychiatrist Erik Erikson, adolescence gives young people the opportunity to stand aside for a while and see how things are shaping up and to devote themselves to discovering their talents and their identity. A welcome way station on the journey from status to status, the institution of adolescence presents youths with a breathing spell before they take on the tasks of full maturity.

Still, contemplation of other societies' reactions to the coming-of-age years seems to tell us that many young people are capable of far greater freedom and responsibility than they have been allowed in our world. Small-scale societies are not usually reluctant to put youthful energies to social use, turning the creativity and imagination released by the onset of puberty to the advantage of the entire community. Instead of delaying the participation of young people in social and economic life, tribal people often present them with challenges that demand the utmost in endurance, mental agility, and good judgment. The enormous contribution that young people have made to society all over the world, and in our own land in the past, suggests that America could make more productive use of one of its most vital resources.

One of the tasks all young people face after puberty is coming to terms with their maturing sexuality, shaping its expression to conform to the expectations of their culture. We consider now the limitations that humans universally have imposed on their sexual impulses. Nowhere is sexuality unrestrained.

Though marriage is universal, it differs from society to society. • A wedding party in Cameroon, West Africa. The party dances on the highway. In order to pass, the traveler must present a gift to the bride.

sexuality limited

4

"So They Would Not Let Me Marry Her"

My doorbell rings: two well-dressed young people are holding out pamphlets. She is blonde, very pretty, has a strong British accent, has traveled all over the world. He is tall, sturdy; Berkeley was not giving him the answers he wanted, so he spent the past two years doing odd jobs, carpentry, waiting on table, and wandering about—until he heard of the Divine Light Mission. Impatiently, they fend off my questions. They are bringing me the word of God. I persist: "Are you married?" She smiles gently; she cannot think of sex until she has achieved perfection. There is a higher love. "You practice chastity?" Again the gentle smile. "The little tree bears no fruit," she says.

Regulating Sex At a time when America is undergoing a vast sexual revolution the response of this healthy young woman may seem unusual. Yet it must be remembered that in all societies sexual restraint rather than permissiveness is the rule. Among the most sexually active of all the higher animals—prepared to copulate in all seasons, climates, and circumstances—humans, nevertheless, impose limitations on themselves by law, custom, religion, or self-denial. The totally promiscuous society exists no more among tribal peoples than it does in Western industrial states.

Societies vary in the degree of restrictiveness that they impose on their members. Some frown on extramarital relations, others on premarital affairs. Some allow one or both. America until recently demanded sexual abstinence outside the institution of marriage. Although they say it in different ways and on different occasions, all human communities say THOU SHALT NOT!

Sex is taboo at times in tribal societies. It may be forbidden not only to the sick but also to their relatives, and in time of epidemic to whole settlements. It may be banned to hunters, fishermen, farmers, warriors, iron smelters, or beer brewers when they are engaging in their duties. It may be prohibited for a long or short time to parents after the birth of their child. Priests, medicine men, and shamans must frequently restrain their erotic impulses. Like the ancient Greeks and Romans, the Cheyenne Indians had their vestal virgins pledged to chastity. Considering the multitude of restrictions, it must be difficult to find the proper time and occasion for sexual activity in a number of tribal communities.*

Sex in the Nursery Left to itself, unregulated sexuality can create chaos in the family, disrupt community cooperation, and interfere with economic activities. Recognizing the tremendous impact of the erotic drive on the individual and the group, all societies begin the sex education of their children early in life. Before they learn to walk, children are already becoming aware of what is expected of them sexually. In one culture they know that touching the genitals is forbidden; in another they know that it is permitted or even encouraged.

*Why should so many taboos be associated with sex? One theory holds that sexual abstinence highlights the importance of an occasion and elevates the position of those who have restrained their impulses. Thus the celibacy of the Divine Light missionaries may be a measure of their seriousness and commitment to their work.

Different peoples teach different lessons. On the island of Alor in Indonesia, parents allow their children to masturbate in public. The Manus of New Guinea, on the other hand, regard masturbation with shame. In America, where the child was once considered a kind of sexually neuter doll, erotic play has been discouraged and sometimes punished.

In many small-scale societies children become sexually sophisticated long before puberty. Parents talk freely about sex in the presence of youngsters who do not have to gather on the street corner or take Physical Education IV to learn the facts of life. A seven-year-old boy of the Wogeo tribe on the northern coast of New Guinea, hearing that women in a neighboring village customarily had intercourse during their menstrual periods, cried, "Disgusting, our women would never do that." In communities where several families are housed under the same roof, children cannot help becoming aware of the most intimate details of the sexual life of both parents and neighbors.

> I, the cricket, have a song.
> I hear the hammock poles.
> I hear the cords creaking.
> I hear my mother having sex:
> Ilaw, kulei, pilaw, pilaw!
>
> —*Xinguano Indians song*

Children's games may culminate in sexual experiences. Arunta boys and girls who play house pretend to have adult sex, and parents interfere only when a "son-in-law" becomes too familiar with a "mother-in-law," a tabooed relationship. By the time boys are nine and girls are twelve, they may end their game in actual sexual union. Initiated boys then turn to older girls, boasting of their conquests as though they were men.

Practices that Americans would label grossly immoral are sometimes viewed as contributing to wholesome child development. According to the Lepcha of northern India, a girl who has not had early sexual experiences will never attain full maturity. The Chewa of southeastern Africa say that children who do not engage in sex should never expect to have babies when grown up. Not all tribal groups are equally tolerant. The extremely puritanical Chiracahua Apache keep the sexes separated from the sixth year on. The Hopi warn their boys that early sexual intimacy will turn them into dwarfs.

Sex Before Marriage A society that looks upon the sexual play of small children with indulgence is likely to allow young people a large measure of freedom, sometimes pushing them into affairs prior to marriage. Before the Spanish Conquest, the ancient Mayans shipped their teen-age sons off to boarding schools where warriors introduced them to the arts of war and prostitutes to the arts of love. Among the Ifugao, a rice-farming people of the Philippines, a bashful son is shamed by his father into having his first affair with a girl. Kaingang Indian parents, rather than reproaching a pregnant daughter, send her to live with one of her lovers. Among the Kadar of northern Nigeria in West Africa, who set no store in premarital chastity, a young man who discovers that his fiancée is pregnant by another man does not reject her, but welcomes her to his bosom. What matters is not the virginity of his bride but her ability—which she has already demonstrated—to bear children.

In the Trobriand Islands off the southern coast of New Guinea parents encouraged their teen-age daughters to take lovers. When visitors from other villages arrived the girls acted as hostesses, offering not only food but their sexual favors to the guests. Nevertheless, when the girls finally married, they were expected to settle down and remain faithful to their spouses for the rest of their lives. Bronislaw Malinowski, the Polish anthropologist who did his field work among the Trobriand Islanders, thought that their sexual code did not encourage licentiousness, but helped a girl select the right marriage partner. A girl who had engaged in a number of premarital affairs could make a wiser choice than one who was sexually inexperienced.

It is not difficult to demonstrate that peoples around the world differ widely in the amount of sexual freedom they allow their young people. But why should one society be more restrictive than another? One answer seems to be that the greatest restraints tend to be found in societies that have classes, castes, or large accumulations of property. In such communities those who have more wealth or prestige than their neighbors may become concerned that their children might marry "below them," and therefore attempt to limit their freedom before marriage. By controlling the sexual conduct of their children, parents hope to control their choice of mates. As a young Kwakiutl Indian of Vancouver, Canada, explained:

"When I was old enough to get a wife my brothers looked for a girl in the same position as I and my brothers had. Without my consent they picked a wife for me. The one I wanted was prettier but she was in a lower position than me so they would not let me marry her."

Who May Marry Whom? No society, no matter how simple, allows its young people absolute freedom of choice in mate selection. All tell their youth who is and who is not a suitable marriage partner. In one community a young man selects his spouse from his own tribe or clan, in another from outside his tribe or clan. In another he must marry a particular cousin. In still another, the sons of one group must marry the daughters of another. Most of the world's marriages are arranged not by young people but by their families or kin. Passion, beauty, love songs, all these may eventually fade, but family interests endure. Or so the oldsters say!

> All your young beauty is to me
> Like a place where the new grass sways
> After the blessing of the rain
> Where the sun unveils the light.
>
> —*Somali African love song*

Marriage is not only the union of two people; it is an alliance of two kinship groups, the young couple serving as the link to hold them together. It does not take Americans long to discover that when they marry the person of their dreams they also are marrying his or her mother, father, grandparents, aunts, uncles, and cousin Matilda from Detroit. In America young people are steered in the direction of their spouses by means of endogamy (Greek: *endon,* within; *gamos,* marriage), a form of marriage that encourages alliances between partners of similar statuses. Only rarely does a humble sailor marry the captain's daughter, as in Gilbert and Sullivan's *H.M.S. Pinafore:*

> I'd like to speak in moderation
> But you have gone too far.
> I'm very sorry to disparage
> A humble foremast lad,
> But to take my daughter's hand in marriage.
> Why, damme, that's too bad.

Most American marriages are contracted between partners who live less than a mile from each other. Contrary to the Hollywood dream, Cinderella will not marry the prince; she is more likely to marry the boy next door. The downtown boys marry the downtown girls; the uptown boys marry the uptown girls. College graduates usually seek out college graduates; whites tend to seek out whites; Catholics, Catholics; and Jews, Jews. Despite the myth that young people are unhampered in mate selection, they commonly make their choice within limitations of class, education, religion, and color. Nevertheless, in America, young people are less hampered in mate selection than in most other Western lands. Marrying outside one's group has been increasing in recent years.

Extramarital Sex In most societies a husband and wife are expected to limit their sexual activities to each other. But the ideal of marital fidelity is often observed in the breach rather than in practice. Some tribal peoples, quite aware that a marriage contract cannot always diminish interest in other partners, have realistically provided for extramarital sex in an institution called wife lending or wife exchange.

A man does not love his wife any the less because she lies with someone else now and then . . . he likes to know about it, that is all; there must be no secrets in such matters.

—A Canadian Eskimo woman

Among the Comanche Indians of the Great Plains of the United States two men entered into a solemn brotherhood agreement under which they shared personal possessions, helped each other out in time of trouble, and on occasion exchanged wives. Quite unlike the present American fad of swinging, in which married couples exchange partners for an evening and often never see each other again, the Comanche custom linked two "brothers" in a permanent bond of kinship and mutual support. Among the Arunta two bands on the verge of armed conflict may temporarily exchange wives in an effort to settle the dispute without bloodshed. Instead of leading to conflict, extramarital sex becomes a means of resolving strife. The Arunta have shrewdly enlisted the human urge for sexual variety in the service of diplomacy.

You may tire of fish but sex is always fun.

—A Xingu Indian

Both simple and complex societies often embrace one code of conduct for males and another for females. The Xingu Indians insist that whereas it is very healthy for a husband to engage in sexual adventures, it is very unwholesome for his wife. A Xinguano who is in the midst of several affairs himself will become enraged if he learns that his wife has been sleeping with a neighbor. Though he may order his wife to sleep with a guest, an Eskimo will murder the man with whom she is having a secret affair. Almost universally people set a double standard in sexual relations: what is proper for a man is often all wrong for a woman.

Homosexuality Every human society promulgates a listing of who and who may not be sexual partners. All forbid relations betwen parent and child, between brother and sister, and between other close kin. Some prohibit relations between members of the same sex. Others, conditionally, accept such relations. American society strongly disapproves of any erotic interest in the same sex, in this respect differing from a slight majority of the world's societies which tolerate homosexuality (Greek: *homos,* same) at least at certain times and for some individuals.

In the Plains Indian culture young men who were incapable of assuming the exacting and dangerous role of warrior were permitted to become *berdache,* transvestites who adopted women's dress and occupations and sometimes married other men. There was nothing shameful about their homosexuality because they were supposed to have taken on their female role in response to the command of a spirit who had appeared during their vision quest. Instead of being scorned, they were admired for their skills in medicine, handicrafts, ceremonials, dances, and the making of love potions. What one society rejects as deviant behavior may be considered socially advantageous in another.

Heterosexuality (Greek: *hetero,* other, different) is the predominant mode of erotic expression throughout the world. And that is just as well, for a society that favored forms of sexuality that did not result in the propagation of offspring could not survive by itself. Yet the definition of heterosexuality often depends on a particular life style. In the United States, for example, a very sharp profile is drawn of manly or womanly conduct. The open display of affection between those of the same sex, especially males, may arouse suspicions of homosexuality. Yet in France no eyebrows are raised when men greet each other with a kiss on each cheek. In Latin America male friends rush into each other's arms with *un abrazo,* an embrace. In Arab lands young men walk hand in hand. Among Australian tribal

The sexual behavior of humans arises from their mammalian heritage and their observations and experience as members of a particular society. • The attitudes, behavior, and feelings of these two young Israelis towards sexuality, courtship, and marriage will be determined in good part by the lessons their society teaches.

people cousins of the same sex stroll with their arms around each other's shoulders. Conduct regarded as perverse in one land starts no tongues wagging in another.

The Regulation of Sex All societies set bounds to the sexual practices of their members both within and outside the marriage relationship. Some are permissive, others quite restrictive. Some are tolerant toward children's sexual behavior; others demand a large measure of propriety of their young people. The degree to which premarital sex is allowed varies from culture to culture. A number of societies accept or even encourage extramarital affairs. Others forbid adultery and severely punish female partners who break the code. In general we can say that groups that are restrictive in other areas in life, such as the control of property, are often also sexually restrictive.

As a result of the sexual revolution America today is far more permissive than in the past. Yet those who fear that current trends will lead to a situation in which anything goes should find reassurance in the innumerable barriers that all societies raise against erotic expression. Everywhere culture specifies the time, place, occasion, and partners for sexual activity. To be human is to restrain the sexual impulse.

We now examine the most universal sexual restraint: the strict prohibition imposed everywhere on erotic relations between close kin.

the incest taboo

5

"What Will I Do for a Brother-in-Law?"

AMID the overwhelming diversity of belief and behavior displayed by humans all over the globe there is one enduring rule on which every society agrees: close relatives may not be sexual partners. Known as the incest taboo, this stringent prohibition against sexual union is observed as solicitously in the Amazon rain forest as in the great urban centers of Europe and the United States.

Kissing Cousins There is no universal agreement, however, as to who are to be considered such close relatives that sex is barred between them. What of first cousins? Some societies regard the marriage of first cousins with horror, much as though they were siblings. Other societies favor such marriages. In Brazil until recently the union of first cousins was considered an ideal marriage among wealthy plantation owners. By marrying each other, cousins who were heirs to the same estate kept the property from being broken into separate parcels.

In many lands a distinction is made among cousins. In a

number of Australian tribes a man is prohibited from marrying a *parallel* cousin, that is, a daughter of his mother's sister or his father's brother. But he is perfectly free to marry a *cross*-cousin, that is, a daughter of his mother's brother or his father's sister.* Though both cousins are as closely related to him genetically, his society defines one as close kin and the other as no kin at all. In the United States, thirty states say No to a man who wants to marry his first cousin, and it doesn't matter whether she is cross or parallel. Twenty states say Yes. What is married bliss in New Jersey is incest in New York.

All peoples agree that parent-child or brother-sister marriages are out of the question. Among the rulers, however, of ancient Egypt, tribal Hawaii, pre-Columbian Peru, and the Azande of West Africa the marriage of siblings was encouraged under the theory that royal personages were not mortals but gods who could marry only fellow deities. Accordingly, Cleopatra of Egypt married two of her younger brothers, though not at the same time. Her godly status did not restrain her from murdering one of them and then bedding down with two earthlings: Julius Caesar and, some time later, his protégé Marc Antony.

Classificatory Kinship Some societies extend the incest ban beyond close kin to include distant relatives and others whom Americans would consider no relatives at all. By means of what anthropologists call classificatory kinship, somewhat distant relatives are called by the same term as very close relatives, so that my father's brothers are called "father" just as my mother's sisters are called "mother." Their female children of my generation will be called "sister." A girl called "sister" must usually be treated as though she were my actual sister and under the rule of incest avoidance I cannot marry her. In some societies everyone in my parents' generation is termed "parent" and

* Cross-cousins are the children of siblings of the opposite sex; parallel cousins are the children of siblings of the same sex.

every one of their daughters is called "sister." It would seem that the only way I am going to secure a mate is by going outside my community.

"Marry Out or Die Out" What use does the incest ban serve? To have been so universally accepted through the ages strongly suggests that it possesses distinct adaptive advantages which make for the well-being and survival of people.

Bronislaw Malinowski has suggested that the denial of sexual access to close relatives evolved among the first humans on earth to protect families from self-destruction. The husband was the hunter of game, the wife the gatherer of small animals and wild plant food, and their survival depended on both their specialized skills and their trust in each other. Sexual competition within the home would have been disastrous. Sons must not contend with the father for the females, nor brothers with brothers. If the family was to survive, Malinowski thought, sexuality had to be brought under strict control. Accordingly, in the course of time, all sexual acts within the family were banned except those between husband and wife. The prohibition became so deeply embedded in tradition that today incestuous relations are everywhere condemned.

But nowhere can families survive by themselves. Especially under tribal conditions of living, families require the cooperation and support of other families in times of danger and often for such activities as harvesting or hunting. According to contemporary anthropological theory the incest taboo acted as the catalyst to bring families together and organize them into larger units such as the band, clan, and tribe.

When young people are barred from finding a mate among close kin they must go outside the home. And when they do, certain adaptive advantages become apparent—as one of Margaret Mead's informants was quick to point out. She once asked an old man of the mountain Arapesh people of New Guinea what he would say to a young fellow who told him that he wanted to marry his own sister. The old man replied:

Few families can survive totally by themselves. In prehistoric times the ban on incest within the family probably compelled young people to go elsewhere to find their spouses and so helped promote cooperation among families. • These women and children are part of a refugee family from the Punjab in India which has joined with seven other families, all of whom are related, to purchase a tractor and begin a cooperative farm.

"What is the matter with you anyhow? Don't you want a brother-in-law? Don't you realize that if you marry another man's sister and another man marries your sister you will have at least two brothers-in-law while if you marry your own sister you will have none? With whom will you hunt? With whom will you garden? With whom will you go to visit?"

The old man regarded incest not as a horrible sin but as a gross error in judgment that kept a man from increasing the number of relatives whom he could lean upon and trust. By channeling his marriage choice away from his home, he acquired not only a wife but also friends and allies. In short, he got himself a second family.

Closely associated with the incest taboo is the rule of exogamy (Greek: *ex,* out; *gamos,* marriage), or the requirement that a person select his mate from outside his kin group or community. Whereas the ban on incest condemns sexuality—except for husband and wife—within the family, the rule of exogamy encourages a person to seek his sexual partner outside his own group. One minimizes disruption within the family, the other fosters cooperation among families.

When a man has one person for his father and another for his father-in-law, friendship extends to a larger number.

—St. Augustine, a father of the Early Christian Church

Exogamy can be a diplomatic game that is played with brides as counters. In some Australian tribes the young men of Band A select their brides from Band B, and the young men of Band B select their brides from Band A, thereby binding the two groups together in a sturdy chain of kinship. The giving of women in marriage, the French anthropologist Claude Lévi-Strauss has said, is the most valuable gift groups can offer one another, for they are giving not only wives but friendship and cooperation. Groups that might otherwise have fought each other to the death join together in larger units for mutual aid.* No less than tribal societies, modern states have also tried to cement alliances by means of diplomatic marriages. Had Philip II of Spain succeeded in his efforts to marry Queen Elizabeth I of England he would have avoided the ignominious defeat of the Spanish Armada and ruled over a joint empire.

It is not unreasonable to assume that the incest taboo coupled with the rule of exogamy arose in response to the need of the earliest humans to organize themselves into social units

* Sad to say, not all societies locate their brides by peaceful means. Some, like the Yanomamö may steal women from their neighbors and thereby ensure a continuous state of feuding and warfare.

larger than the family. The denial of incestuous mating avoided conflict within the domestic group and at the same time minimized conflict with other groups by compelling young people to seek sexual satisfaction outside the family. Love and affection once confined to the immediate members of the family could now be extended to strangers.

Stretching the incest ban among tribal peoples to include distant relatives or even those who are not relatives begins to take on meaning. Young people in search of mates are forced to go outside their community; and the further afield they go, the wider the network of in-laws and allies grows. (A number of California Indian tribes insisted that their women find a husband who spoke another language.) We may speculate that the earliest families of humanity could not have survived unless they joined together in clusters held together by exogamous unions. Faced with the alternative of "marrying out or dying out," prehistoric peoples "chose" to marry out.

The Incest Ban in the Industrial State But how are we to account for the persistence of the incest taboo in technologically advanced societies? Survival in America does not depend on the support of a wide circle of relatives outside the home. My brother-in-law may be a precious asset in a simple society, but in the industrial state the role he plays in my life is often no more significant than that of a tennis partner or a fourth hand at bridge. My principal safeguards against disaster are not my wife's kin but my unemployment insurance, the local police, and the hospital. What use does the ban on incest serve today?

The American sociologist Talcott Parsons suggests that complex societies derive economic and other advantages by diverting sexual drives away from the home. A child's first love relations are with its parents and siblings. Were he to continue such close relationships into adult life, he would become attached to the family group rather than to the larger society. If he is to punch a time clock, shop at the supermarket, pay his income tax, and generally maintain his place in the modern industrial world, the individual must break the emotional chains that bind him to his natal family. By channeling his sexual impulses toward strangers, the incest ban gives him the impetus to find not only his bride but also his economic and social role outside the home.

The Genes Say No Another theory offered for the persistence of the incest taboo is that the mating of close kin constitutes a serious health hazard. In very early times people gradually became aware that brother-sister and parent-child unions produced genetically inferior offspring and therefore forbade such relationships—setting a precedent that has been followed by all societies to this day.

It is true that close inbreeding can result in genetic effects. A small population of isolated people burdened with hemophilia, cretinism, or other inherited maladies who mate among themselves are likely to produce a large proportion of handicapped children. However, another small inbreeding group that did not start out with such genetic disadvantages would probably have normal offspring for many generations. Small hunting bands in which the marriage of first cousins is customary are notably free of hereditary diseases. Inbreeding itself would not seem to cause degeneration of offspring but to intensify the inheritance of good or bad traits already possessed by the breeding group. Whatever might be said of her morals, Cleopatra was a remarkably sensual and intelligent woman who did not exhibit any of the ills said to accompany inbreeding. And yet she appears to have been the direct descendant of twelve generations of brother-sister marriages. Was she just lucky?

Nevertheless, because inbreeding does intensify the inheritance of undesirable traits already in the parental stock, the prohibition of the mating of close relatives makes good sense, just as compulsory vaccination or clean air regulations do. We may speculate that should the day ever come when all hereditary diseases have been eliminated, then incest avoidance—at

least as a public health measure—would become obsolete. When that time comes, according to American anthropologist Marvin Harris, the marriage of close relatives would become a legal though rare alternative to exogamous mating. In the meantime brothers-in-law are in little danger of becoming an endangered species.

Now I am the father of dogs.

—A Dakota Indian, learning of the incestuous union of his son and daughter

Of all the higher animals humans alone avoid union with close kin. It is likely that the foundations of human society were laid when the incest ban was adopted in prehistoric times. The guardian of harmony within the family, the taboo allowed children to grow up trusting and unmolested. Compelling people to seek mates outside the family, it encouraged strong alliances for defense, ceremonials, and food gathering. Everywhere incest avoidance helped preserve the unity of the family and at the same time extended the areas of social and economic cooperation.

We have not yet defined the family. Its definition, we will discover, changes in time and space, depending in good part on the culture in which we live.

Exogamy is the practice of marrying outside a culturally defined group such as a family, caste, class, band, or tribe. Members of the large agricultural communities in Israel called kibbutzim will usually seek mates outside their own settlements. • A kibbutz wedding in Israel.

all in the family

6

"But Without the Family We Are Nothing"

RECENTLY in a Long Island college town a group of students rented a house on a street zoned for one-family living. The neighbors quickly protested and took the students to court. A family, the plaintiffs said, was a group of closely related people consisting of a father, mother, and their children. By no stretch of the English language could the students be called a family. The defendants replied that such a definition was out of step with the times. A group of people unrelated by blood who come together under the same roof for common household purposes could now be considered a family. New life styles demanded new definitions.

Ultimately the court ruled against the students. The traditional definition of a family was safe, at least on streets zoned for one-family living. Nonetheless, the concept of the family has been changing. America's most sacred institution, the cornerstone of the social order and the bedrock of national values, is under serious challenge.

The Nuclear Family Until the 1970s few Americans would have had any difficulty in defining the family. It is what anthropologists call a nuclear family, consisting of an adult male and an adult female together with their immature offspring. If one of the adults is missing, the group is described as a broken family. If there are no offspring, it is called an incomplete family. Grandparents, maiden aunts, or children by a previous marriage, though they happen to reside within the same household, are not considered full-fledged family members.

The citizens who fought the student incursion into their neighborhood would be pleased to learn that the nuclear family is the predominant domestic arrangement around the world. It is found not only in highly industrialized lands but in tribal and peasant societies; it thrives as well in the Arctic tundra or the South American rain forest as in the suburbs of Long Island. We may reasonably suppose that an institution so widely diffused and occurring in so many different societies must possess adaptive advantages for its members.

> What is a man. A man is nothing. Without his family he is of less importance than that bug crossing the trail. If he had no one he would be killed by his enemies. He would be poorer than a newborn child. In the white way of doing things the family is not so important. The police and the soldiers protect you, the courts give you justice, the post office carries messages for you. Everything is taken care of, even your children if you die. But without the family we are nothing.
>
> —*A Pomo Indian of California*

The Sexual Division of Labor In many simple societies the nuclear family produces almost everything its members require in order to live. Like the manorial fief in the Middle Ages or the American farm in pioneer days, it is the basic unit of the economy. It is a poppa-mamma business that farms, hunts, gardens, gathers, fishes, builds, weaves, and sews.

Each of the adult members assumes specialized jobs suited to his or her abilities. The female generally takes on tasks she can perform while caring for or nursing the children such as preparing food, gardening, fetching water, and cleaning the home. The male—heavier musculatured and unhampered by

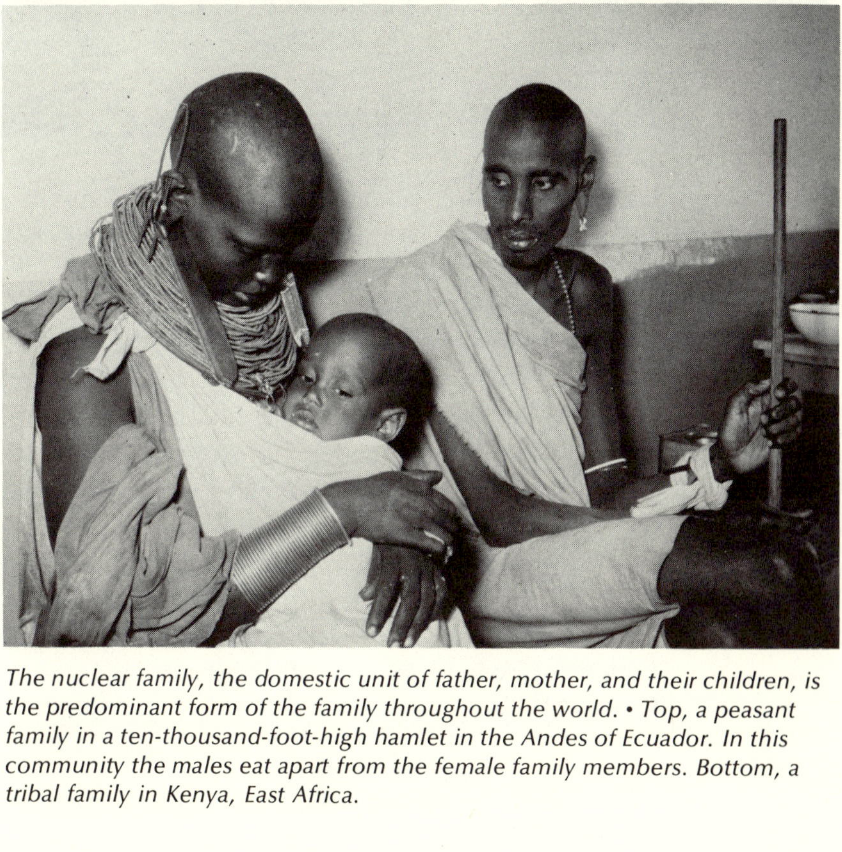

The nuclear family, the domestic unit of father, mother, and their children, is the predominant form of the family throughout the world. • Top, a peasant family in a ten-thousand-foot-high hamlet in the Andes of Ecuador. In this community the males eat apart from the female family members. Bottom, a tribal family in Kenya, East Africa.

By dividing family work on a sexual basis husband and wife gain great facility in their assigned tasks. Among the Eskimos women are charged with the making of clothing. • An Eskimo woman softens a hide with her teeth before making it into a garment.

the demands of pregnancy or nursing—becomes the hunter, deep-sea fisherman, herder, plowman, and warrior. Survival often depends on the unique skills of both husband and wife. An Eskimo husband provides the game, but the wife manufactures the clothing that permits him to hunt the game. The wife may be sexually attractive, but if she cannot chew and sew hides, the family will not withstand the Arctic climate. "A man is the hunter, but his wife makes him," the Eskimo say.

> For want of food or gruel, life will not depart
> Owing to cold or wind, life will not depart
> Owing to rain or dew, life will not depart
> But if there is no wife, life will depart.
>
> —*Song of the Vedda people of Ceylon*

Only by belonging to a family can a person be assured of the necessities of life. Singles may flourish in a technologically advanced society, but in a tribal community they are rare.

Division of labor by sex has also been characteristic of Western families. The twentieth-century American wife has usually performed her tasks within the household, the husband in an office or factory outside the home. In recent years, however, labor-saving machinery and frozen foods have lightened the burden of household duties so that while the children dine on pizza from the freezer many wives are organizing garage sales, returning to school, or taking up a career once more.*

In all societies the family is the principal agency for the care and protection of the young child. Of all the higher mammals the human has the longest period of infant dependency. Around the planet the family meets the child's physical needs, provides him with love and affection, gives him his first lessons in the values and rules of his group, and influences the course of his future life.

> It is so still in the house
> There is a calm in the house;
> The snowstorm wails out there
> And the dogs are rolled up with
>   snouts under their tails.
> My little boy sleeps on the ledge.
> On his back he lies breathing
>   through his open mouth.
> His little stomach is bulging round.
> Is it strange if I start to cry with joy?
>
> —*An Eskimo Mother's Song*

The nuclear family provides another vital service. The human female is continuously available for sexual activity and the human male is continuously interested. By giving the male frequent access to his mate, the family deflects the social

* See page 114 for the changed role of women today.

disruption that could follow an unrestrained scramble for sexual partners. We may reasonably imagine that in early times the institution of permanently paired mating helped reduce competition for females and ensure social tranquility.

The nuclear family apparently is an ideal domestic arrangement, providing for easily accessible heterosexual relationships and for the care of offspring resulting from the union. It permits both sexes to share the economic burden effectively; it replenishes the population, trains the children for their future adult roles in society, and safeguards social order. Nevertheless, there are domestic arrangements different from the one male, one female plus offspring model that supply similar services with at least equal satisfaction to their members. Before we consider them, let us take a closer look at the American family.

The American Family Usually restricted to the mated couple and their immature offspring, the American family with an average membership of three plus is perhaps the smallest domestic group on earth. When the children are of marriageable age they usually depart from the natal home and set up households of their own, contrary to the practice in the majority of the world's cultures where young people continue to reside after marriage under the parental roof or in quarters close by. Reduced to two elderly adults the American family lingers on until the parents die or, by reason of age or other incapacity, take refuge in a nursing or retirement home. Once the parents are gone, the family they headed vanishes. A temporary association, it springs into being with the marriage of the parents and ends with their death and the dispersal of their offspring and property.

During its early and middle years the American family is often on the move, changing jobs, schools, and residence, shifting from neighborhood to neighborhood, from city to suburbs and back again, from the North to the sun belt, from the East to the West. Hundreds of thousands live in mobile homes.

The American nuclear family is limited in both membership and duration and endures for no more than the parents' lifespan. Once the children are grown and departed, the elderly face increasing insecurity. Some end their days in old-age and nursing institutions. In nonindustrial societies the elderly often become part of the family of one of their married children. • An elderly Rengma Naga of northeast India wears a warrior shawl.

My mother lives in the East, in Maryland. My father is dead; I have two sisters and they live in Texas. There are many old friends; they live in Baltimore, Chicago, Minneapolis, Seattle, Boston, Vancouver, and Albuquerque, places like that. . . . We regularly send Christmas cards to each other.

—*Dr. John A. Crane, pastor of the Unitarian Church of Santa Barbara, California*

Unlike young people in nonindustrial communities who grow up among a host of relatives, American children usually live apart from grandparents, uncles, aunts, and cousins. In nine-

HOW MANY OF YOUR RELATIVES DO YOU KNOW?

Highly mobile and living apart from most of their relatives, Americans today know fewer kin than their grandparents did. A 1955 survey of college students indicated that they could recall about 30 relatives each.

On the average, of their own generation they knew 10.9 relatives, of their parents' generation 11.1, of their grandparents' generation 7.5, of their great-grandparents' generation 1.7, of their nephews and nieces' generation 1.6.

teenth-century America, especially in rural areas, relatives tended to cluster in the same village or town. The elderly were often housed with the family and helped take care of the young. Today relatives are often widely scattered over the country. Kin living halfway across the continent may hesitate before coming home for a family reunion. Young people appear to know fewer relatives than their parents or grandparents did.

A visitor from another society would look in vain for the tools, equipment, or place of business of the American family. Unlike the family in the majority of the world's societies, the American model usually does not farm, manufacture, or render services for sale. It is a consuming, not a producing, unit. A housewife may grow tomatoes or zinnias in her backyard, but for most of her food, clothing, and household goods she goes to the supermarket or the mail-order catalog. Traditional household tasks such as cleaning, washing, and food preparation are often transferred to outside agencies. The education of the young, a vital function of the family in nonindustrial socie-

It is an extended family that usually consists of the husband and wife together with their children, together with grandparents and one or two brothers- or sisters-in-law, all of whom work on the family farm. • Indonesian family, Worogiri, Semarang.

ties, may be taken over by baby sitters, day-care centers, camps, schools, and the television screen. Even infant nursing may be assumed by a stranger equipped with a bottle of bovine milk formula.

In families in small-scale societies all the members of the family, including young children, contribute their labor and skills to the support of the household. Because a father's work is in the home or close by, he can easily pass his skills on to his children. The American father, on the other hand, is a night visitor who at the end of a long day at the factory or office may be more inclined to watch the Jets or Knicks on TV than to interest his offspring in his work. In industrial societies the job and the home are in different worlds.

Unencumbered by aged parents or a large body of kin, the American family can be highly mobile, following the job trail to an adjoining city, Alaska, or Saudi Arabia. "Have skills; will travel" is the motto of thousands of workers who go wherever opportunity beckons. Their primary allegiance is not to the elders and family tradition but to their career. What some might consider weaknesses of the nuclear family, such as its smallness or its isolation from relatives, enable it to serve the industrial society swiftly and efficiently.

You plant a tree and never see it grow.

—An American executive who has lived in seven different cities in ten years

The Extended Family The nuclear family seems admirably suited to the social and economic needs of contemporary Western communities. Yet it is also present among some nomadic tribal bands such as the Eskimo who must break up into small family units at certain times of the year in order to hunt game and gather other forms of wild food. The industrial state and the hunting and gathering economy could not be more widely divergent, and yet they have at least two features in common. Both cultures rely on mobility, the industrial worker pursuing a job and the hunter chasing game. Neither culture requires for survival the kind of land ownership that endures from generation to generation.

Where a sedentary way of life and long-term ownership of land is required, as in farming societies, the typical domestic unit is the extended family. Consisting of two or more nuclear families, an extended family is a group of relatives who live together in a common household. In the traditional Chinese family, three generations lived together under the same roof: the elderly father and mother, their unmarried children, and their adult sons together with their families. A daughter married into another family, but a son brought his bride to live in his parents' house.

A son's first allegiance was to his parents, toward whom he was expected to show more concern than to his wife. In their presence he had to refrain from speaking to her or even expressing his feelings about her welfare. Such parental domination of grown children is typical of extended families. Among the Tajputs of northern India, a mother continues to feed her married son as though he were still her small boy. Among the Barotse of Zambia in Africa a young husband who paid less attention to his parents than to his wife was believed to have been bewitched by her.

In China the source of all authority and wisdom was the elderly male parent who presided over the farm and the family and arranged his sons' marriages. When a father died, the eldest son replaced him as head of the domestic unit and took charge of the estate, which was owned by the family in common. The death of parents rather than bringing the family to an end gave it a new lease on life. The children become the elders and in turn passed the land and its traditions on to their children. Unlike the American nuclear family, which ends with the death of the parents, the extended family is touched with immortality.

An economic unit that produces almost everything needed for subsistence, the extended family is adapted to the needs of

The typical extended family consists of three generations living within the same household—grandparents, parents, and children. It may also consist of two or more siblings, their spouses, and their children. • An extended family in Iran.

a stable agricultural society.* While the nuclear family in the industrial world sends its children out of the home to earn their living and start their own domestic units when they marry, the extended family holds some of them within the natal residence all their lives. The extended family has little place in a society like America, where in a single year 40 million people may change their home address.

* Still, the extended family can also be found in an urban setting. In the modern city of Karachi in Pakistan, an extended family may occupy a six-story house, the elderly parents residing on the street level and the youngest son and his family on the top floor. Though the grown children may be professionals who go to their office every morning in another part of the city, they faithfully turn their income over to their father for the benefit of the entire family. They will probably never leave their ancestral home.

In an economy based on the cultivation of the soil, the presence of the extended family prevents the subdivision of the land into ruinously tiny plots. Since there are no separate heirs, the estate can be handed down intact from generation to generation. Self-perpetuating and owning all property in common, the extended family is a form of insurance against economic disaster.

The Commune The nuclear family in America may serve modern society by encouraging the development of independent-minded people capable of selecting their own marriage partners, causes, and careers. Does it equally serve the emotional needs of people? Some Americans look back with nostalgia to a time when many people lived in small towns and villages surrounded by a large body of relatives with whom they shared their work and their outlook on life. Would it be possible at the present time to create a domestic unit that would restore the sense of community and security that was supposed to be characteristic of American families in the past? Among the alternative family forms that have been suggested is the commune, an extended domestic group whose unrelated members live in the same household and share the work and property.

> And all that believed were together and had all things in common and their possessions and goods, and parted them to all men as every man had need.
>
> —*Acts 2:44, 45*

The commune is not new in American history but stretches all the way back to Colonial times. In the nineteenth century religious sects such as the Shakers lived communally, treating each other like members of a close-knit family. In 1841 Nathaniel Hawthorne joined Brook Farm, a communal settlement in Massachusetts that combined farm and school. He wrote at the time: "We have left the rusty iron framework of society behind; we have broken through hindrances powerful enough to keep many people on the weary treadmill of the established system." Hawthorne, however, soon rejoined the established system, for Brook Farm, like many communes then and now, was a short-lived experiment.

Communes became very popular in the 1960s when some young people deserting their natal households came together and attempted to create their own version of the family. While some "grooved" with nature in trees and shacks, smoked "grass," and waited for a check from home, others tried to live like Jesus and His Disciples by serving the poor in inner-city ghettos. Some built their communes around a small business or farm, made bricks, ate organic food, raised chickens and goats, and revived old American handicrafts.

> Our aim is to live without money, to abolish it altogether. We'll bake our own bread and make our own clothes and help each other. If we have children they will be the responsibility of the whole group. The way we see it the family system is old-fashioned and past. It's time to start doing things in a different way more like the early Christians who shared everything with each other.
>
> —*A barefoot girl in Golden Gate Park, San Francisco, 1972*

Some communes achieved a reputation for promiscuity by sharing not only their members' possessions and labor but also their sexual favors. But general sexual accessibility frequently gave way to traditional pairing, probably because it is difficult for humans to maintain ties of trust and intimacy with rotating partners.

Other communes were eminently respectable, maintained a low image on a quiet street in a good suburb, kept the hi-fi down, avoided late parties, and tended the lawn as carefully as the traditional American family next door.

Of the communes founded in the sixties one of the most successful has been The Farm, located forty miles outside of Nashville, Tennessee in Lewis County. Almost one thousand members live on the commune's seventeen-hundred-acre farm. Most of the adults are married and live in bungalows which are shared by general families. They spend their day in teams working for The Farm. Both men and women take part in the daily work, pooling their labor and receiving what they need from the commune's commissaries and bank. They have their meals in a common dining room.

> If you live on the Farm you give the Farm everything because the Farm is going to take care of your needs. So if you have to go out and do something in town that takes money you stop at the [Farm] bank and if there's bread the bank lady will give you some bread and you give her the change when you get back.
>
> —Hey Beatnik! This is the Farm Book, *by Stephen Gaskin. The Farm, Summertown, Tennessee*

There is no casual sex, homosexuality, coffee, alcohol, meat, or drugs other than marijuana. Sex roles are sharply defined. Administration, leadership, and manual work are the specialties of the men. Food preparation, household maintenance, and the care of the children are the tasks of the women. A religious association, The Farm tries to give its members the sense of closeness and community they claim to have missed in their own natal families.

The Kibbutz In the United States alternatives to the conventional family such as the commune are generally looked upon with hostility and suspicion. In the state of Israel the *kibbutz* (Hebrew: a gathering or company) is a respected way of life for a portion of the population. An agricultural settlement often located at the frontier between Israel and hostile neighbors, the kibbutz is a cluster of nuclear families that own and produce property communally.

In some kibbutzim each married couple lives in a bed-sitting room and eats in a common dining room. Their children are raised by professional nurses and teachers, first in an infant's house and later in a children's house, seeing their parents for an "hour of love" each day. As the children grow older they

A kibbutz is an invented extended family in Israel whose members pool their resources and property. In the nuclear family the spouses work for each other, dividing the labor between them. In the kibbutz husband and wife work for the larger economic unit. The rearing of children, a prime responsibility of the family throughout the world, is transferred to professional teachers and nurses.

see their parents for longer periods but return to their dormitory each evening before curfew. After graduation from high school, two young people may decide to share a common room, a sign that they wish to marry. The marriage ceremony, however, does not usually take place until after the birth of their first child.

Kibbutz members do not see themselves merely as farmers who have pooled their resources and labor, but as members of the same extended family. Parents, ideally, regard all the children of the settlement as though they were their own. When young people come of marriageable age they will generally go outside their kibbutz to find a mate. Familiarity apparently breeds sexual disinterest.

Polygamy The kibbutz is a deliberately invented family intended, in part, to meet the demands of a beleaguered pioneering society in which parents, unhampered by child care, can be ready to put down the plow and pick up the gun. Like other forms of the family, invented or natural, it serves the social, cultural, and economic needs of its member. But what of the polygamous family (Greek: *poly,* many; *gamos,* marriage), a domestic arrangement based on the union of three or more spouses? What purpose outside of sexual variety does it serve?

Polygamy comes in several sizes and shapes: a single husband married to several wives, a single wife married to several husbands, several husbands married to several wives. The only large-scale attempt to institutionalize polygamy in the United States—by the Mormons in the Utah Territory in the 1850s—was ultimately outlawed by the Supreme Court. "To advocate plural wives offends the common sense of mankind," declared the justices. They were unaware that polygamy gave no offense to millions of people throughout the globe.

Though a polygamous union can land a spouse in jail in America it is acceptable in over 70 percent of the world's societies. Yet though plural marriages in a particular society may be permitted or even encouraged, most adults will have to remain content with a single spouse if only because the number of males and females available for marriage at any one time is usually about equal. (Among the early Mormons only about 20 percent of the adult males had more than one wife.) He who takes more than one wife may very well keep a neighbor single. On the other hand, several polygamous societies have gotten around the difficulty and made a sufficient number of brides available for plural unions by lowering the marriage age for females or by preventing the young men of the community from seeking a wife until they reach an advanced age.

> Polygamy . . . appears to be on the increase in the American West despite the fact that the practice is illegal. There is no accurate count of American polygamists but 20,000 to 30,000 seems a realistic figure. . . . A Salt Lake County prosecutor said, "If we prosecuted all the people [in Utah] who lived in sin the jails would not hold them. Such prosecution today might be held unconstitutional on grounds of freedom of religion."
>
> —*New York Times,* 1977

Polygyny Polygyny (Greek: *poly,* many; *gynē,* woman) is the form of polygamy in which a single husband is married to several wives. Among the mountain Arapesh, who cherish brothers-in-law so much, a man who takes two wives doubles the number of valued in-laws. With two wives assisting him he can grow more food in his garden. If one wife is away, his home will still be tidy and his meals on time. And he will not be denied a sexual partner when one wife is ill or nursing a newborn infant.

The advantages of polygyny are not confined to the husband. A young married Arapesh woman was talking to Margaret Mead about her co-wife. "My best friend," she beamed, "two by two we go for water; two by two we gather firewood; two by two we dye our skirts." A second woman in the home can supply both household help and companionship. She can also provide a neat answer to the question of who will take care of the kids when her spouse and co-wife are out for the evening.

Polygynous marriages are not always rosy. Children of different mothers may vie for the attention of the one father. Jealous wives often gossip, quarrel, and compose nasty songs about each other.

> Woman, thy soul is misshapen.
> In haste was it made, was it made.
> So fleshless a face tells that
> Thy soul was formed without care.

Three-quarters of all societies on earth permit family arrangements other than the one husband–one wife unit. Even though a society may permit polygamy, most marriages will be monogamous. Even among the early Mormons in the United States only a minority of families had plural wives. • A polygynous family in Dakar, Senegal, West Africa.

> The ancestral clay of thy making
> Was moulded in haste, in haste.
> A thing of no beauty art thou,
> Thy feet unsuited for feet,
> Thy face unsuited for face.
>
> —*A co-wife's song in Dahomey, West Africa*

A Cheyenne Indian woman once hanged herself when her husband brought home a younger and more attractive co-wife. Her own grandmother, however, was more philosophical: "Why kill yourself over such a little thing?" she said. Polygynous communities try to confine conflict over "such a little thing" in a number of ways. In some societies a husband selects as his wives sisters, who will usually get along better than nonrelatives. Sometimes a husband is required to adhere to a schedule, scrupulously visiting each wife in turn for the same length of time. Elsewhere an oldest wife who is no longer the sexual favorite is permitted to boss the younger women around.

In the Western world polygyny stirs up visions of voluptuous half-naked women segregated in harems guarded by eunuchs armed with scimitars. But "harem polygyny" is a special case limited to the nobility of the Middle East. Far more widespread is "hut polygyny," a domestic arrangement in which each wife, often with independent means of her own, lives with her children in her own house within a compound (Westerners tend to designate homes in primitive regions as huts which in their own land they would call bungalows or cottages). The husband has his own quarters where his wives take turns caring for him and sleeping with him. Among the Yoruba of southwest Nigeria, an agrarian society of 12 million people, many co-wives are economically independent, owning real estate, monopolizing retail trading, or running buses called mammy wagons. Women who have achieved a large degree of civic and economic independence are no more degraded by polygyny than by any other form of marriage.

Is there any relationship between polygyny and infant health? There may well be. Anthropologists have noted that tropical peoples who live on low-protein foods such as taro, sweet potato, banana, and breadfruit tend to have extended taboos on a husband's having intercourse with his wife after childbirth. (We recall the Arapesh husband who had to observe such a taboo). These societies also tend to be polygynous. After childbirth a wife will have at least a year or two before she is again pregnant. Her child will thereby receive the protein in mother's milk that would otherwise be missing from his diet. It is reasonable to assume that a husband who can approach other wives sexually is not likely to break the taboo. The custom of polygyny accompanied by the prohibition on intercourse after childbirth apparently safeguards the health of children by warding off protein deficiency illnesses.

Polyandry Polyandry (Greek: *poly,* many; andr-, man), is the marriage of one wife to several husbands, a union far less frequent than polygyny. Among the Todas—who introduce the newborn babe to the world at dawn—a girl at puberty becomes the wife of both her fiancé and his brothers. The brothers share the one wife apparently without conflict or ill feeling. When a brother is in bed with the wife, he places his mantle and staff outside the door as a sign that the others should not intrude. On the birth of her first child the wife is presented with a symbolic bow and arrow by one of the brothers, who thereby acquires the right to call the newborn his own, together with the next two infants the mother bears. Thereafter, a second brother presents the bow and arrow and becomes the father of the next set of children.

Fraternal polyandry, the sharing of one wife by several brothers, is sometimes found in southeastern Asian societies in which only males inherit land. Were each brother to set up his own household, the portion of the family property he would inherit might be too small to provide a living for his family. By marrying one wife and thereby maintaining only one household, brothers keep their expenses down and their inheritance intact. In a few East African communities a man may ask his brothers to contribute cattle for the price of his bride. All the brothers are then entitled to live with the bride until she bears her first child and thus becomes the sole wife of her husband.

Group Marriage Can other combinations of marriage partners be imagined? If so, they have probably been tried somewhere on earth. For example, there is the very infrequent institution of group marriage, or the union of several men and several women, all of whom have sexual access to each other. The Todas sometimes bring a second wife into the household, and she is shared by the brothers as they share the first.

Among the Polynesians of the Marquesas Islands in the western Pacific a headman presided over a cluster of buildings set on a platform along the shoreline. The larger and more elaborate the buildings and platform, the greater was his prestige. To recruit the staff he needed to maintain this huge complex, he married an attractive woman with an entourage of several lovers who moved in with her and joined the headman's household as laborers and secondary husbands. As he became more ambitious the headman took on additional wives along with their admirers. All the husbands, at least in theory, had equal sexual access to all the wives. Group marriage made good business sense for the headman.

Nayar Marriage Whether monogamous or polygamous, marriage usually requires a husband. But in several family patterns the male spouse is all but nonexistent. The Nayars are a warrior upper caste in the state of Kerala in India. Until one hundred years ago the custom was to marry seven- to twelve-year-old girls in a single mass ceremony to soldier bridegrooms selected by the local astrologer. Thereupon, a bridegroom went off on his military duties without having relations with his bride and usually never saw her again.

When the girl reached puberty, she began to receive lovers who would appear after supper and leave early the next morning. Should a lover notice another's weapons at the door, he would wait or return at a more auspicious time. A child born to a Nayar girl was considered legitimate, provided that one of her lovers paid the midwife's fee—usually a few vegetables and a piece of cloth. Though called the father of the child, the lover assumed neither the support of the household nor any of the burdens of parenthood. Instead, the care and protection of the young woman and her children fell on one of her own brothers, who like his fellow warriors never settled down with a wife.

Throughout the world families are often held together by the conjugal link, or the tie between husband and wife. The

Nayar family, however, was tied together with a consanguineous link, or the relationship of blood between mother and children. From the universal drama of family living the Nayars removed one of the principal actors, the father-husband, substituting a mother's brother as the protector and provider. An arrangement adapted to the needs of mercenary soldiers who could be called away at any time, the Nayar marriage assured both mother and children a permanent home and the support of a male relative.

A domestic unit found at the present time in both Europe and the Americas bears some relationship to the Nayar model. In the matricentric family the father is absent or only an occasional visitor, and the children are brought up by their mother and her female relatives. Matricentric families may exist among the urban poor of Europe such as Scottish coal miners, in the black ghettos of the United States, and in broad areas of the Caribbean and Central and South America. An adaptation to extreme poverty, the matricentric household tends to appear when fathers are incapable of supporting their families and mothers become the economic mainstay in their place.

Woman Marries Woman Asked to define *marriage,* we might say, "Marriage is a socially approved economic and sexual union between a man and woman intended to be permanent." This is a definition which may be fine and dandy for our Western culture, but which would hardly be relevant to the Nayars or many other peoples. In Dahomey, Africa, marriage may involve a union of two females. A wealthy older woman wanting children but having none of her own may marry a young woman and then arrange for her bride to become pregnant by a man she designates for her. Since the older woman is legally the spouse of the bride, she becomes the parent of any offspring resulting from the mating, and the children call her "father."

There is no imputation of lesbianism in such an arrangement, which may produce a sound and permanent family. Aside from the odd feature of woman marrying woman, the custom has something in common with child adoption procedures in America in which a married couple submit to a long legal ritual to become the parents of a child they themselves did not conceive.

In a number of African tribes the mother of a son who died early in life before he had any children may arrange to have his ghost married to a girl she has selected. The girl then mates with a stranger and their offspring become the heirs and children of the dead son—much to the delight of the "grandmother."

What we are seeing is biological parenthood giving way to sociological parenthood. Among some African peoples a man becomes the father of his own children only after he has given a bride's price, usually in the form of cattle, to his father-in-law. Should he fail to pay the price, the children become his father-in-law's. As the Thonga people say, "Cattle beget children." What matters is not so much who is the biological father but who is the person socially recognized as the father. Thus a "father" might be a husband in the Nilgiri Hills of India who presents a symbolic bow and arrow to a shared wife, a wealthy older woman in Dahomey, an American who possesses the proper adoption papers, or a ghost. Our culture designates whose children we are.

Marriage can be a device to acquire not only parenthood but property, rank, and titles. In America marriage may give a bride a vested interest in her husband's property. In Europe it may give a spouse a title of nobility. A commoner in England named Philip Montbatten became Prince Philip by marrying Queen Elizabeth.

In like manner among the Northwest Coast Kwakiutl Indians a century ago a commoner could acquire noble rank by marrying the daughter of a title holder. Even if no daughter were available, the title seeker was not deterred. He married the left foot or the right hand or some other part of the body of the title holder. It did not matter that there was no bride; what mattered was the transfer of title. The Kwakiutl used marriage to pass prerogatives and privileges from one person to another.

The Licensing of Parenthood Each human society throws a halo around its own perception of social custom, often regarding the point of view of other groups as bizarre or strange. Americans and other Western peoples, for example, conceive of marriage as the union of two people of the opposite sex for the principal purpose of instituting a family, and it strikes us as odd that others should see marriage as a neat device for child adoption or title transfer. But if we step outside the bounds of our own life style for a moment, we may be able to accept the thought that marriage need not be the union of a single man and a single woman; it need not be the union of a living person with a living person; it need not be the union of persons of the opposite sex. How then shall we define it? Leaving aside the difficult case of the Kwakiutls, we may say that marriage is the institution in most human societies that legitimizes children—and quickly leave it at that. It tells us whose children are whose. Or as Malinowski put it: "Marriage is the licensing of parenthood."

Just as the many variations on marriage around the world cannot be contained within the American model, so many families refuse to fit into the ideal of a household comprising Pa, Ma and the kids. In only one out of every four societies on earth is the nuclear family the only permissible domestic arrangement. The union of two adults of the opposite sex living under the same roof with their offspring is just one of a number of successful family patterns.*

Like a complex living organism, the family is a remarkably resilient and sturdy institution which modifies its shape, size, and characteristics to meet wide variations in the social, eco-

* For the variations on the theme of "Home, Sweet Home" that Americans have recently begun to play, see page 74.

nomic, and natural environment. The only unchangeable element in the family seems to be the bond between mother and children. Within an appropriate setting humans have been able to satisfy their sexual, emotional, educational, and economic needs though they share a multiplicity of spouses, eliminate the conjugal relation between male and female, or invite scores of grandparents, uncles, and aunts to find shelter under the same roof.

Can we imagine education without schooling? In most simple societies the family and not an outside institution is charged with the training of the child. We will now look at communities in which children are educated without benefit of professional instructors, grades, classes, or courses of study.

tribal education

7

"When I Am a Man, Then I Shall Be a Hunter"

IAN HOGBIN, the Australian anthropologist who lived among the Wogeo of New Guinea, was talking to a father who had just presented a garden to his two-year-old daughter. "You are quite right," her father said, "she is too young to do the work. But her mother and I will say to her, 'This is your ground,' and soon she will understand. When she is a little older she will plant the seeds we now plant for her."

Education without Schooling Hogbin noticed that Wogeo children learned adult tasks at an early age by watching their parents. A four-year-old, imitating his father who was planting taro, began to make holes in the soil. His father smiled indulgently: "There, put your fingers this way, hold the stick like this and you'll dig without hurting your back." The boy worked diligently and after a while ran off to show his sister how to dig. Then they both got busy with a pretend garden of their own.

A parent hard at work building a canoe urged his son to help though the boy's efforts got in his way. "If I send him away," he told Hogbin, "how can I expect him to know anything? Today he is a nuisance but one of these days he and I will fashion a canoe together." When the boy built a coconut shell canoe, the father could not have shown more concern than if the child had fashioned an actual boat. "Your sail is too small to take advantage of the wind," he said. "Your outrigger is unwieldy."

By the time a Wogeo boy is four or five he is taken on his first fishing trip. At first he goes only for an hour and then only on a cloudy day to avoid sunburn and seasickness. As he grows older he receives lessons in navigation and quickly becomes an expert boatman and fisherman.

An American, asked where he received his education, might reply, "At P.S. 48; at DeWitt Clinton High School, and at City University." A Wogeo youth might say, "From my parents, from my playmates, from the elders of my village." Unlike the student in technologically advanced societies who depends on formal educational institutions, the Wogeo youth relies on his family and community for the skills and knowledge he will

My grandmother wanted me to have an education so she kept me out of school.

—*Margaret Mead*

require in his society. Like the majority of people on earth he does not receive his education in school. And yet by the time he is an adult he is as well equipped to get along in his culture as an American university graduate is in his.

What is Education? One of the basic purposes of any society is to train the child to behave, feel, and think in ways acceptable to his culture. Unlike a lower animal whose responses are in good part genetically programmed, a child must be taught what is considered the proper manner of eating, talking, worshipping, or making love. In addition to absorbing the life style of those around him, the child must also learn to repeat some of the behavior of past generations so that he will speak

In the industrial state the child of four or five is separated from his family for a good part of the day and sent to a special institution called school, where he is taught by strangers, who are bound to him neither by kinship nor sacred obligation. For him, education means what happens in school. • An elementary school class in Japan.

the same language, pray to the same gods, support the same form of government, and cherish the same values as his ancestors. It is by means of education that culture is transmitted from generation to generation.

In a simple society a parent expects his child to follow in his path, become what he is, and do what he does. Tribal education provides an unbroken continuity from the past to the present and to the future. In an industrial society such as the United States a parent often hopes that his child will become

Schooling in the industrial state may help a child attain a higher status than that of his parent. In the nonindustrial state, education prepares the child to carry on the same work as his parent. • An artisan at work in Madina in Sfax, Tunisia, North Africa. Note how the craftsman has found additional "hands" for his work.

what he never succeeded in becoming. A poor industrial worker dreams that his son will study hard in school, graduate with honors, go to law school, and one day hang his coat in the cloakroom of the Senate of the United States. Education in America, by helping the child achieve a higher social and economic status than that of his parent, becomes a mechanism of change for at least some portion of the population. Different societies make different demands on education.

Education encompasses not only the formal training we acquire in school but also enculturation, the process by which we absorb the ways of thinking, feeling, and behaving of our people. We become enculturated by identifying with our parents, by rewards and punishments, and by exposure to the traditions, myths, and rituals of our society. As we achieve new statuses in life such as adulthood, parenthood, or old age we gain new skills, attitudes, and ideas. Schooling, on which Western peoples place so much emphasis, is only one aspect of a person's lifetime education.

> By the age of six the average child will have completed the basic American education and be ready to enter school. . . . From television he will have learned how to pick a lock, commit a fairly complicated hold-up, get laundry twice as white and kill people with a variety of sophisticated armaments. From watching his parents the child will already know how to smoke, how much whiskey to mix with soda, what kind of language to use when angry and how to violate the speed laws without being caught.
>
> —*Russell Baker, American journalist, 1975*

The Open Classroom In small-scale societies education takes place in an open classroom which may be a clearing in the forest, the village esplanade, or the family hearth. Unsegregated from adult life, the child has plenty of opportunity to observe the ways of his elders. Listening to their uncensored conversations, joining in their rituals, or tagging along on their hunting, gathering, and fishing expeditions, he receives his ed-

A child's education begins in his mother's arms and includes enculturation, the process of conditioning and training whereby people acquire their culture. Long before a child is of school age, he learns a thousand nuances of his culture from the way he is bathed, carried, nursed, encouraged, played with, cuddled, fed, sung to, and talked to. • Top, this Rajasthan mother from Mysore, India, who is working on road construction must carry soil on her head and her baby on her arm. Bottom, the way this infant from Liberia on the west coast of Africa is reared will deeply influence her subsequent patterns of behavior.

ucation under circumstances American children would regard as a prolonged vacation.

Wogeo children are shielded neither from talk of sex nor death. Little that is unpleasant is withheld from them. When a death occurs they are not shunted aside but brought to the bedside of the dying elder, who will if possible reserve a few words of farewell for the little ones. American parents prepare a child for adult life not by immersing him in grown-up experiences, but by sending him to school. Tribal parents keep the child in their company and consider him not so much a child as a developing, if incomplete, adult. That children in small-scale communities should seem exceedingly precocious to outside visitors is not surprising.

The curriculum in tribal societies is the life the child sees going on about him. The subjects he learns and the skills he acquires are those for which he often has an immediate use. The paddle he learns to carve is soon used at sea. The mask he learns to make is worn at a dance. The songs he learns are sung at the next festival. The fish he learns to spear are eaten at the next meal. His studies are not abstractions but techniques for survival. He will not flunk any of them.

Play is enlisted in the service of education. An Eskimo father gives his toddler a puppy, a little harness, and a tiny sealskin whip. Soon the boy is driving the puppy harnessed to a toy sled about the igloo. Later he learns to make a real harness and crack a whiplash ten to fifteen feet long over a team of dogs. By the time he is twelve the boy is accompanying his father on walrus hunts, trudging all day long behind the sled no matter how bitter the weather. For Eskimo girls too, play gradually shades off into work. At first they make clothing for their dolls, cutting the pattern and chewing the skins just as their mothers do for adult wear. Later they mend their own boots and help make the mittens and stockings for the entire family. In industrial societies play has little economic significance except for the youngster who is going to become a professional ball player. In tribal communities play prepares a child for lifework.

When I am a man, then I shall be a hunter.
When I am a man, then I shall be a harpooner.
When I am a man, then I shall be a canoe builder.
When I am a man, then I shall be a carpenter.
When I am a man, then I shall be an artisan.
Oh Father, Ya! Ha! Ha! Ha!

—*Kwakiutl Indian children's song*

In all societies education involves the teaching of values. "Make certain that those who visit this household leave it with full bellies," a Wogeo mother says to her seven-year-old. A father pulls two scuffling boys apart: "What, would you strike a kinsman? Do you think that a boy you hit is going to like you?" The war-like Yanomamö Indians, on the other hand, may teach children to be cruel and ferocious by forcing them to fight each other.

Values are also taught by means of tales, legends, and myths. A story about a witch is not only entertainment but also a lesson in what a society considers good or evil, clean or unclean, right or wrong. The more perverse the behavior of the witch, the greater the pressure on the listener to avoid such conduct. Since no one, including the storyteller, doubts the reality of such tales in tribal communities, the effect on a small child can be overwhelming.

Teachers in Tribal Societies Although no one is trained for the profession, there is never a shortage of teachers. A child need only look about to notice the master of every art, craft, or

In technologically advanced societies the schools bear the principal burden for the formal education of the child. In tribal and peasant societies the responsibility rests primarily on the family. However, as small-scale societies become Westernized, their pattern of education approaches the industrial model. • Top, today in some parts of New Guinea compulsory school attendance is as rigorously enforced as it is in the United States. A chemistry class at the Technical Training School in Rabaul. Bottom, a class in a remote village in Upper Volta, West Africa.

Burning
Rusting of iron
Air
Water
Vaseline
Boiled water
Cotton
anhydrous

In small-scale societies girls learn on the job by helping parents with household tasks. • These girls from Gunung Kidul in Java, Indonesia, take care of their small brothers.

skill practiced in his community. Basket weavers, carpenters, canoe builders, or painters of masks—all are in residence every day in the week, ready to offer instruction to children. The teacher does not usually face a group but a single learner who is given as much time as he needs to master a task. No stranger to the child, the teacher is customarily a close relation or a neighbor.

A mother's brother who is a noted fisherman teaches his nephew how to tell when the fish are running. An indulgent grandfather offers instruction in ancient history by singing of the deeds of the great heroes or of the duties of the gods. Among the Maori, the Polynesian people of New Zealand, elderly relatives taught table manners as well as the traditions of their people and took the children to great feasts to hear the orators and see how village affairs were conducted.

Bush Schools Not all tribal societies lack schools. In western Africa a number of secret organizations conduct schools for teen-age boys and girls that resemble summer work camps in America. Among the best known are those of the Poro societies of Sierra Leone.

When a boy enters a Poro school he goes through an initiation rite in which his skin is lacerated with a hook to represent the imprint of the Poro spirit which has supposedly swallowed him. At the end of the school session he will be expelled from the monster and returned to life. The boys camp in the wilderness where they grow accustomed to hardship. They sleep on pallets of sticks and water-soaked bedding and are awakened at dawn each day. Impossible tasks are demanded of them and they are punished when they fail. Formal instruction includes road building, drumming, basketry, acrobatics, clothing making, and native customs.

On the last day of the school term each boy, after his head has been shaved, is immersed in a stream and then given a new name and a new suit of clothes. Their skins gleaming with palm oil, all the boys under the cover of a huge canopy march into

To the small child in Western society, a father's work consists of dashing from the house in the morning and returning in the evening. In a small-scale community the father's work is usually close at hand. The child learns not by absorbing abstractions such as the multiplication table, but by directly engaging in adult tasks. • In Tocuaro, Mexico, the local wood-carver teaches his craft to his son by guiding the boy's hand.

town where parents, relatives, and friends greet them and shower them with gifts to commemorate their "return to life." After four days of feasting and celebration the current Poro school session is officially closed.

Among the Maori, adolescent boys were sent away to winter schools for instruction in house building, navigation, farming, and weapon making. The sons of priests and chiefs, however, were enrolled for three to five years in boarding schools where they studied the "three baskets of learning": (1) traditions, genealogy, and military history; (2) religion and ritual; and (3) black magic.

Before graduating a student of the "three baskets" was confronted with a series of examinations that culminated in a supreme test of his mastery of the black arts. His hair ritually cut, he was led to a shrine in front of which stood a man whom he was to slay merely by uttering a spell. Usually a slave was selected for the test. If the candidate, however, was the son of a great chief, the victim might be a member of the nobility or even a close relative. Surprisingly the victim often fell dead, probably because he had been poisoned a short time before. Duly impressed with his power, the young graduate was now ready to venture out into the world to try his magic against any who displeased him.

Suffering, Fright, and Outrage Compared to Western education which frequently neglects the emotions to concentrate on words and abstract ideas, learning in a tribal setting may be associated with feelings of awe and wonder. A Mayan child working alongside his parents in the cornfield spoke in a hushed tone because the land was a temple sacred to the gods. He learned not only the techniques of gardening but the incantations that assured a successful harvest.

Suffering, fright, and outrage may be employed as teaching techniques in the course of initiation rites. All year round the threat of drought and famine troubles the Hopi Indians of the American Southwest. To persuade the gods to send the life-giving rain, dancers called *kachinas,* dressed in brilliantly colored costumes and carved masks, perform in the village square from sunrise to sunset. The children are told that the dancers are not human beings but gods who will send rain if all the boys and girls keep a good heart, that is, behave properly.

The time comes when a Hopi boy is initiated into the *kachina* society. He is conducted into the *kiva,* or underground ceremonial chamber, where the *kachinas* appear, suddenly turn on him, and lash him with yucca whips. Though his godfather holds him close and takes some of the blows himself, the child feels the sting of the whips. Then at last the whipping stops and the *kachinas* remove their masks. To the child's shame and astonishment the creatures smiling benignly on him are not gods at all; they are mortals like himself, relatives and neighbors whom he has known all his life. He has been cruelly tricked.

> I recognized nearly everyone of them and felt very unhappy because I had been told all my life that the kachinas were gods. I was especially shocked and angry when I saw all my uncles, father, and clan brothers dancing as kachinas. I felt the worst when I saw my own father—and when he glanced at me I turned my head aside.
>
> —*A Hopi Indian*

The mortification and shock soon pass. He is left with the realization that he is no longer a small child, for he now knows a secret that only grown-ups know. Yes, the dancers are only human, but the gods they impersonate are real. Let him therefore keep a good heart and the gods will bring rain and his people will prosper. Until this time he has only been an observer watching the masked dancers. Now he must take his place among them as he will shortly take his place among the adults of his community. The mask of the gods has descended on him.

Culture and Education The aims and methods of tribal education have enabled people to maintain their own life styles for thousands of years. Despite three waves of conquest—the Spanish, the Mexican, and the American—the Hopi have securely held to many of their ancient customs, values, and religion, a testimony to the strength of their system of education. At a time when American education is on the firing line and many schools are troubled by low academic standards, poor discipline, high dropout rates, and student apathy, it is tempting to look favorably upon other ways of education for a solution of our current problems.

But tribal educational practices no matter how attractive

they may seem within their own setting cannot be transplanted into a vastly more complex culture. For one thing an industrial society requires long periods of sophisticated training. The skill required to manipulate a digging stick can be mastered in a few hours, the education required to program a computer may take years. To understand the complexities of contemporary civilization the student must learn not only what is immediately useful to him or what is related to him closely in time and space but also much that is far removed, whether it is ancient history, *Hamlet,* the Revolutionary War, or nuclear fission. And since the scope of knowledge is so great, no parent, elder, or dedicated teacher can ever impart all that a young person should know.

Benjamin Franklin tells the story of a group of philanthropic gentlemen who kindly offered a number of scholarships to the University of Virginia to Iroquois Indian youths. Whereupon they received the following reply from the chiefs of the Iroquois:

"Several of our young men were brought up in your colleges but when they came back to us they were bad runners, knew neither how to build a cabin, kill an enemy, take a deer or speak our language. They were fit for neither warriors, hunters or counsellors. They were totally good for nothing. We are nonetheless obliged for your kind offer to educate our sons though we decline accepting it, and to show our grateful sense if the gentlemen of Virginia will send us a dozen of their sons we will take care of their education, instruct them in all we know and make men of them."

A system of education, like other aspects of culture, will usually make sense only within the environment that gave it birth.

Both in and out of school young people in almost all societies are taught that women are by nature inferior beings compared to men. Let us explore the implications of this worldwide myth.

the status of women

8

"If the Woman Gets Fancies in Her Head, She Must Be Beaten"

AMONG the Mende, a tribal people of Sierra Leone in western Africa, the godmother of a female child comes for the infant three days after birth and takes her outdoors. Turning the baby toward the morning sun she spits in her face and cries: "Resemble me in all my ways and deeds for you are named after me."

One way the baby can resemble her godmother is to behave in a manner appropriate to her sex. In every human society the child is taught to conform to its sex role, the distinctive pattern of behavior that depends on whether one is male or female. A boy must behave like a boy, a girl like a girl.

Sexual Conformity In all lands lessons in sex roles begin early in life. Among the Hopi Indians a little girl is told she will be a cook; a little boy is told he will be a runner. Girls are encouraged to play at grinding corn and making pots, the boys at farming, herding, and horseback riding. Among the Tallensi, a people of northern Ghana in West Africa, the girls play at preparing food. They carefully examine the "flour," add the right amounts of water, stir, and finally serve the "porridge" just as their mothers do. Boys imitate their fathers, pretending to hunt animals and care for cattle.

To bear the club, carry the spear,
Fight, storm the fortress, kill,
Climb the mountain, ride the waves,
Grow food, build canoes,
Make mats.

—*Maori nursery song for boys*

To grow food,
To gather shellfish,
To weave garments,
To bear a burden.

—*Maori nursery song for girls*

In America children are entertained with fairy tales in which their sex roles are clearly set forth. Males sally forth into the great world, slay dragons, decapitate witches, climb beanstalks, and engage in other equally bold and enterprising ventures. Females are generally passive and withdrawn, staying indoors until a prince rouses them from a hundred-year nap or fits their dainty foot with a glass slipper.

Tribal or technologically advanced, all peoples agree that men and women should exhibit behavior appropriate to their sex. But since anatomy alone cannot guarantee that a child will follow his assigned sex role, each society must reinforce biology with lessons in sexual conformity. Children are therefore taught to feel at home with the kind of play, work, clothing, hair arrangement, gestures, language, and manners deemed proper for their sex. In southern Egypt children learn that men walk down the middle of the street; women stay close to the wall. In the Trobriand Islands boys quickly learn that they are not to carry burdens on their head even in jest. Only females carry burdens on their head. In America boys are not encouraged to play with dolls. Parents in all societies constantly remind children of their sexual destiny.

I don't think a boy should have a doll because it will send him on the wrong road to being a man.

—*A fourth-grade American boy*

Sex Roles and Culture Almost all humankind agrees that male conduct and female conduct should be different. This does not mean that all societies agree on what is appropriate conduct for males and what is appropriate conduct for females. In America boys traditionally don't cry. In Wogeo, however, *girls* don't cry. A girl who cries is not considered a real girl. A mother says in mock surprise to her weeping daughter, "Tears from a girl. Why perhaps she's a boy after all. She will be growing a penis next." From society to society there is a remarkable flexibility in what is expected of each sex.

In her study "Sex and Temperament in Three Primitive Societies" Margaret Mead said that the traits we call masculine and feminine are "as lightly linked to sex as are the clothing, manners, and the form of head-dress that a society at a given period assigns to either sex."* She observed that among the Tchambuli of New Guinea the women were the business people of the community, doing the fishing and manufacturing the mosquito netting which was sold to other tribes. The men, on the other hand, plaited baskets, painted masks, played the flute, danced, and shopped. Unlike the women the men gossiped, bickered, and fell in and out of friendships. While the women shaved their heads and wore no makeup, the men spent their time fussing and arranging their curls. And in lovemaking, it was the women who went after the men.

Have the Tchambuli allotted the wrong traits to the sexes in defiance of human nature? Though not as dramatically as the Tchambuli, other cultures around the world also challenge Western assumptions of what constitutes proper male and female behavior. In Ghana in western Africa women control a

*Almost certainly an overstatement. It is very likely that a number of traits are sex-linked; that is, they are determined not only by cultural conditioning but also by the differing body structures and hormonal balances of the two sexes.

good part of the economy. They own trucking lines and fishing fleets and conduct almost 90 percent of the retail trade of the country. Among the Zuni Indians of the American Southwest, women contend for the love of a man in no-holds-barred fist fights.

All societies arbitrarily assign traits to one sex or the other. What one people consider normal male or female conduct will be condemned as deviant by another. The behavior of the sexes is determined not only by physical differences but by cultural and historical forces. American notions of what is proper female conduct have changed over the past two centuries. In pioneer days women worked side by side with their men, driving the prairie wagons, plowing the fields, and fighting off the Indians. In the last decades of the twentieth century the Victorian stereotype of the soft, clinging, helpless female is rapidly giving way to woman as independent, outspoken, and sturdy. Sex roles reflect changing social and economic conditions.

> They told me that as a woman I'd never get into graduate school in physics, so they got me a job at the College of Physicians and Surgeons and promised that, if I were a good girl, I could take courses there. Then I got an assistantship in physics at the University of Illinois and I tore up my steno notebooks.
>
> —*Dr. Rosalyn Yalow, Nobel Prizewinner in medicine, 1977*

Men's Work and Women's Work In all human societies men and women do different work. What is a male monopoly in one society, however, may be a female monopoly in another. To the Navajo Indians, spinning and weaving are woman's work. To their Hopi neighbors such tasks are distinctly man's work. Among the Iroquois Indians farming was assigned to the women. Among the Pueblo Indians farming was for men only. In the United States most doctors and almost all truck drivers are male. In the Soviet Union most doctors and most truck drivers are female.

The work of each sex varies from society to society. Nevertheless, there are a few tasks which all peoples assign to the same sex. Almost everywhere soldiering, policing, and governing, as well as big game hunting, herding, weapon making, metal working, and the manufacture of musical instruments have been male specialties. Almost everywhere women have been the rearers of small children, the carriers of fuel and water, the gatherers of plants, and the collectors of small wild animals. In general men engage in work involving risk and spatial mobility, women in work that does not interfere with pregnancy, lactation, and infant care.

Assigning an occupation to one sex rather than another, at least in tribal societies, has adaptive value. Since males typically can run faster, club harder, and hurl a spear farther than females, it makes good sense to turn defense and big game hunting over to them. A community in which women were primarily responsible for hunting and fighting would jeopardize its chances of survival. It is also reasonable to allow females to handle household tasks, since such work can be done in connection with the feeding and care of the young. In like manner other duties that can be performed in the vicinity of the household such as the manufacture of clothing, pots, and baskets may also become the domain of women. A community with a simple technology improves its manner of living by linking certain tasks to one sex rather than the other.

Although women are generally assigned to homemaking tasks in tribal societies, they can also be successful in what are usually considered male specialties. In northern Australian tribes women are the hunters of kangaroo. In many societies they carry far heavier burdens than males. A mountain Arapesh woman can carry a seventy-pound load suspended from a band around her forehead up a steep muddy mountain slope with a nursing baby at her breast. (Arapesh males say that women's heads are harder than men's.) Among the Yahgan Indians who live along the icy shores of Tierra del Fuego, women are better swimmers than men. In general tribal women work harder than males, thereby giving them time to loaf, raid their neighbors,

Traditionally, the tasks assigned to women in small-scale societies are those they can perform while taking care of their young. • Top, a mother and daughter pound millet into flour in Matourkou, Upper Volta, West Africa. Bottom, a mother collects water for washing and drinking in India.

and boast of how much stronger they are than their wives.

Look at me, look at my arm. I have plowed and planted and gathered into barns and no man could get ahead of me and aren't I a woman? I have worked as much and eat as much (when I could get it) and bear the lash as well and aren't I a woman? I have borne thirteen children and seen em most all sold off into slavery and when I cried out with a mother's grief none but Jesus heard and aren't I a woman? Den that little man in black dar he say that woman can't have as much rights as man cause Jesus w'ant a woman. Where did your Christ come from . . . ? From God and a woman. Man had nothing to do with Him.

—*Sojourner Truth, black female abolitionist* (*1797–1883*)

The differences between men and women's strength and stamina have been grossly exaggerated. As women begin to compete with men in sports, belief in innate female physical weakness becomes more difficult to maintain. In 1975 in the grueling twenty-six-mile New York City Marathon a woman came in ahead of all but 25 of the 488 men in the contest. Before that time women had been barred from the marathon on the ground that they might hurt themselves.

On Marlin Rig No. 2, Gulf of Mexico—"Ralph" rises at 5 A.M., climbs into greasy overalls, laces up steel-toe shoes, plops on a hard hat, eats breakfast and begins a 12-hour workday that often stretches into 16, 18, or even 20 hours. It's hard work. There are 50-pound and 100-pound sacks of dried drilling mud to pile and unpile. There are supply boats to unload, cables to splice, bulkheads to sandblast and paint, and 800-pound sections of drill pipe to handle. "Ralph" is a roustabout—a drilling-rig workhand. Her real name is Cindy Meyers. She is 20 years old.

—New York Times, *1976*

The Inequality of Women Almost everywhere men have dominated politics, religion, and the economic sphere. Men have been the authorities, potentates, dictators, popes, chairmen of the board, and tribal chieftains. Festivals and rituals, pomp and circumstance, uniforms and badges, have legiti-

In many tribal and peasant societies young girls work while their brothers are still playing. • Top, in Borneo a young girl has the task of carrying water home in long bamboo tubes. Bottom, on the streets of Cliza in Cochabamba, Bolivia, this Indian girl of five already has a job—leading a blind man.

mized their ascendant position. When a woman has gained the spotlight, it has usually been in the part of understudy.

> If we are to be the providers, then we must be the masters. And if the woman gets fancies into her head, then she must be beaten. That will bring her to her senses.
>
> —*An Eskimo male*

There are a number of societies in which women have come close to equality with men. Among the Iroquois the women owned the cornfields, controlled food distribution, and had veto power over the selection of the chiefs who nevertheless were always male. Among the Hopi, women own the houses, furniture, fields, and the harvest. Divorce is at their discretion. A man may return home after a hard day's work in his wife's fields to find his paint pots, his dance shirt and sash, his second pair of moccasins, and his other personal possessions piled up at the doorsill. He takes the hint and goes back to his mother. Yet though women have authority in the family, they are not the most influential members of the Hopi community. The eldest son in the family becomes the clan priest and leader, not his sister.

The subordination of women to men has always been characteristic of human societies. Tales about matriarchies, communities in which women were the dominant sex, are without historical basis. With few exceptions it has been a man's world.*

Every culture must provide for the programming of women so that they will accept their subordinate role with more or less grace—like ladies. In American television commercials girls observe females washing shirts, polishing floors, cleaning toilets, and shopping for groceries. They also observe males walking the girders of skyscrapers, making astonishing discoveries in

*American parents in common with parents around the world usually prefer sons to daughters. In only five small societies are girls wanted in preference to boys.

laboratories, and probing the surface of the moon. When she was three Jennifer noticed that while her father was away at work her mother was at home shopping, cleaning, and cooking. Learning that her mother once held an outside job, she asked wide-eyed: "Were you a man?" She was already absorbing the lesson that a man's domain is the great world; a woman's, the household. Women have not been where the action is. But sex roles are changing, and Jennifer, now aged six, discovers that there are women bricklayers, women bus drivers, women forest rangers, women police officers, and women mountain climbers.

Until very recently American schools continued the indoctrination in sex roles begun at home. In arithmetic problems males weighed concrete, measured bridges, drove trains, while females poured cups of flour and laid out dress patterns. In history men fired the shot heard round the world and signed the Declaration of Independence. Betsy Ross made a brief appearance—as a seamstress.

Sexism, or the discriminatory treatment of people on the basis of their sex, limits their aspirations and primes them to expect less of and for themselves. At the age of nine in America boys and girls have achieved approximately the same academic scores. By the age of thirteen, however, females have begun a decine in achievement, except in the languages and the arts, which continues into adulthood. Female high school graduates who enter college with excellent records usually set their vocational goals more modestly than males. It is far safer to become a teacher, dietician, or nurse than to attempt to break into fields traditionally reserved for males such as mathematics, politics, diplomacy, or banking.

Polled on how much money they would sue for in case they lost their eyesight in an accident, male college students asked on the average, $50,000. Female students asked, $20,000.

New York Times, *1976*

In Western societies the difference in the physical strength of the sexes has often been exaggerated. In technologically undeveloped communities women perform tasks that require great strength and endurance. • A female road-building crew in Lesotho in South Africa.

Carrying a load of sugarcane, a woman walks across a bridge on Togo on the west coast of Africa.

The Emancipation of Women Under primitive conditions of living, allotting tasks on the basis of sex has survival value. In the pursuit of big game hunting or hand-to-hand fighting the extra measure of power and endurance provided by males lends validity to the sexual division of labor. Western industrial society, however, demands the strength neither to bring down a charging bison nor to overcome an enemy by brute force. Power tools, automation, and sophisticated weaponry cancel whatever advantages male strength may provide in pre-industrial communities. A forklift can be run as efficiently by a ninety-pound female as by a two-hundred-pound male. By steadily decreasing the usefulness of sheer muscle power, technology is destroying whatever legitimacy male domination ever had. The machine is sexually blindfolded.

"When they need you, you can do anything." • *A U.S. Naval pilot checks the gear of a tracker anti-submarine aircraft.*

At 39 years of age Mary Maynard . . . works the day shift driving a 48 ton truck for the Pittston Coal Company along this region's potholed roads. And last week she was elected president of the United Mine Workers Local, 1791.

—New York Times, *1977*

It is not surprising that the demand for sexual equality should arise in complex industrial societies or that the struggle for the emancipation of women should have attained its first victories in the United States, the most technologically developed nation in the world. In the 1970s the American women's liberation movement, with the support of a democratic tradition that proclaimed that all were created equal, helped to tear down barriers of discrimination in career choice, employment, advancement in employment, education, sports, and religion. Changes in sexual attitudes, values, and behavior that had endured for centuries took place almost as the nation watched.

The first woman to head a police precinct in New York City was named yesterday by the police commissioner. . . . Captain Vittoria Renzullo graduated first in her class at the Police Academy.

—New York Times, *1976*

What relevance does the women's liberation movement have outside the industrialized countries of the world? More than half of all females on earth live under desperately poor conditions, without running water, refrigeration, adequate shelter, central heating, or protein-rich food. Boys are favored above girls. When there are shortages of food boys receive more to eat than girls. If schooling is available boys receive it before girls. By the age of four or five girls are already saddled with adult tasks, carrying water, fetching firewood, and caring for babies.

She wakes at 5 A.M., eats little or nothing, straps her baby on her back and walks a mile to a field. There for ten hours she bends or stoops, planting or hoeing. At 3 P.M. she scavenges for firewood and carries it and her child back home. There she pounds grain into meal and prepares other food. By 6 P.M.

In India until a few years ago women in rural areas were confined to the home. Today, young women such as these bicyclists are organizing village women's clubs and teaching reading, nutrition, and sewing to adults.

she is ready for another walk, this time a three mile round trip to fetch water. She is a woman in rural Zambia but she could also live elsewhere in Africa, Latin America, or Asia . . . her life represents the lives of more than a billion women, the majority of the world's female population.

—*United Nations World Conference on Women, 1975*

But if sexual inequality were abolished overnight, the result would only be shared misery for men and women. Until the lot of all people is improved in the underdeveloped regions of the globe, changing the status of women will not produce decent living conditions. In most of the world's societies the basic

As Western culture is diffused and rural societies are drawn into the world market economy, some women begin to achieve a measure of freedom and independence. • A policewoman in Lagos, Nigeria, West Africa.

Where people live close to starvation, raising the status of women would be of little benefit. • This family lives south of the Sahara in the Sahelian Zone, a drought-stricken region. Millions of cattle have perished and one-third of the human population suffers from hunger and malnutrition.

problem is grinding poverty not sexual discrimination. In South America, Africa, and Asia where resources are scarce and caloric intake low the eloquent advocates of sexual liberation encounter stubborn resistance. Solutions that satisfy the people of one society make little sense to those whose needs are different.

One sexual image many of us have about women is that they are inherently peace loving and gentle. But what of males? Are they not by nature pugnacious, violent, and warlike? From the sorry record of many human societies for cruelty, massacre, torture, and fighting we might think so. In the next chapter we deal with violence and war in large-scale and simple societies. We begin with a curious experiment at Yale in the early 1970s.

violence and war

9

"I Am Not Going to Kill That Man"

RECRUITED by an advertisement in a New Haven, Connecticut, newspaper, a volunteer enters a psychological laboratory at Yale University. Here he encounters a man dressed in a grey laboratory coat who asks him to cooperate in a scientific experiment to test the effect of electric shock on learning. The volunteer is to administer a verbal test to a student strapped into a chair with electrodes attached to his wrists. Every time the student misses the correct answer, the volunteer is to give him an increasingly severe electric shock. If the volunteer consents to the experiment, he is seated before an impressive "shock generator" on which there are thirty switches, the last of which is labeled "450 volts: DANGER, SEVERE SHOCK." The explanations completed, the man in the grey coat retires to the side and the volunteer throws the first switch. At 75 volts the student in the chair grunts. At 120 volts he lets out a shriek. At 150 he cries, "Let me out of here, let me out of here!" The volunteer is troubled: Shall he continue? The man in the grey coat answers severely, "The experiment must go on." And the volunteer continues right up to the switch marked "450 volts."

He can't stand it. I'm not going to kill that man. You hear him hollering. He's hollering. What if something happens to him. . . . You know what I mean. . . . You mean I have to keep on going up the scale. No sir, I'm not going to kill that man. I am not going to give him 450 volts. . . .

—A volunteer in the Milgrim experiment

The Milgrim Experiment Did this experiment actually take place in America? It was in fact an elaborate hoax. The "shock generator" was a stage prop gussied up with blinking lights and buttons; the "student" in the chair was a confederate who simulated pain when the appropriate switch was thrown. His cries were tape recordings. The man in the grey coat was also a part of the script. Only the volunteer was an innocent. Before the experiment was over more than one thousand people from all walks of life in New Haven—housewives, blue-collar workers, college professors—had revealed how easily they could be induced to inflict pain on other people. No one who answered the advertisement ever refused to participate. Less than one-half of all the volunteers balked at reaching for the 450-volt switch. Even when informed that the student had a bad heart, a number still persisted in going on to the end.

The Milgrim experiment (named after its originator) seems to say that once people are convinced by some authority—in this case a man in a grey coat, surrounded by the reassuring artifacts of science—that what they are doing is proper, they are likely to put aside compassion and decency and behave in an inhuman way. Are people naturally cruel and violent? Is it only the policeman on the beat who keeps most citizens within the bounds of decent behavior? Violence, according to the popular wisdom, is part and parcel of human nature, a killer instinct inherited from brutish Old Stone Age ancestors.

Man is a predator whose natural instinct is to kill with a weapon.

—Robert Ardrey, American writer

Aggression and Nonaggression If any people illustrate an apparently natural propensity for cruelty and violence, it is the nomadic Kaingang Indians of the highlands of southern Brazil. Until they were herded into a reservation in recent years they were among the most ferocious people on earth, vicious not only toward their enemies but toward each other, domestic animals, and even trees which they irrationally slashed with their axes. They loved recounting past murders and old feuds, remembering with gruesome precision the cries of the assailants, the wounds of the victims, and the details of the weather. Once a murder had occurred the killer, like Macbeth, could not rest but must wipe out the entire family of his victim, including the children, lest a single survivor hunt him down. A hunter who went after game by himself feared those he had left behind. Were they angry with him? They must want his death and he therefore must strike first. Murder was the way a clever man kept alive. And so the Kaingang slept fitfully, staring into the treacherous darkness, keeping the memories of past slaughter fresh with tales of revenge and bloodshed.

But for people like the Kaingang whose life style is crowded with aggression, there are others like the Semai who are remarkably gentle. The Semai, a group of central Malaysian tribes who live by farming, hurt neither humans nor animals. Rather than kill a chicken he has raised, a Semai will sell it in a distant village. Children who squabble are immediately removed from the scene of dispute by their parents. Since adults never exhibit violence, a would-be aggressive child has no models to emulate. Confronted by force, a Semai will merely become passive or turn away. A man who has had too much to drink may become talkative but almost never angry or hostile.

The mountain Arapesh, another gentle people, cannot tolerate quarreling. Suppose that a man has an argument with his wife. All the males in the village take up their flutes, go to the offender, and play him out of his house. Then they litter the floor with leaves to register their disapproval of his outrageous conduct.

The Arapesh are so mild in disposition that it is difficult to find anyone to assume the post of "big man," or village leader.

"Big men" are expected to talk loudly, strut about, and boast of their deeds. Since no Arapesh would normally behave in such an aggressive manner, people must be educated for the role. Two boys in their early teens are selected to be *buanyin,* or exchange partners, and trained to be nasty toward each other. "What, you have no pigs, no yams. You have no friends, no relatives. You have never given a feast. Were you born headfirst like a human being?" says one to the other, provoking him to reply in kind. Their basic gentleness deprogrammed, the boys grow up to be leaders capable of ordering the rest of the community around. The Arapesh must undergo long periods of indoctrination before they can be anything but peaceable and cooperative.

The ferocity of some peoples and the gentleness of others suggest that the expression of violence varies enormously from society to society. Where one group is quick to anger, pugnacious, and cruel, another may be mild, passive, and peace loving. If a killer instinct is buried in the genes of humankind, people like the Semai and mountain Arapesh have somehow managed to avoid inheriting it.

An occasion that provokes a furious show of violence in one community may be passed over lightly in another. Among some peoples a husband who discovers his wife engaged in an extramarital affair kills the other man. A Xinguano spouse usually doesn't do anything more than give his unfaithful wife a good whack or two. A Hopi husband, confronting his wife's infidelity, contemplates not murder but divorce.

A man with a good heart will pay no attention if he found his wife misbehaving with another man. He would just take his things and go back to his own home.

—*A Hopi male*

Around the world violence often does trigger further violence. In many small-scale societies the victim retaliates by injuring his assailant. Nevertheless, people who have suffered in-

The Xingu Indians of central Brazil are a peaceable people. Their principal sport, wrestling, is practiced according to precise rules which prohibit any display of anger or hostility.

jury frequently turn to other alternatives such as song contests. Among the Tiv, a tribal group living on the Guinea coast of West Africa, an injured person gives a series of beer-drinking parties at which the guests sing scurrilous songs about the offender, who responds in turn by staging a number of his own all-night concerts. When it looks as though the rival entertainments are going to end in a free-for-all, the village chief steps in and adjudicates the case on the basis not only of the facts but of the quality of the beer and the singing.

The Eskimos may also seek retribution through singing rather than violence. Appearing before a large public gathering the parties to the dispute take turns singing insulting songs. The audience responds with yelling and derisive laughter and eventually drowns out one of the litigants who is then declared the loser.

Rather than embracing violence, people will at times go to extraordinary lengths to avoid it. The relatives of a murdered Eskimo instead of seeking vengeance sometimes take the killer into the family to become the husband and support of the woman he widowed. In a somewhat similar custom the Navajo levy a fine against the murderer and turn it over to the family of the victim as compensation for their loss. Tribal Australians, as we have noted, may turn from shedding blood to swapping wives. What began as a fight-in ends as a love-in.

Even the Yanomamö Indians—who give their four-year-old sons lessons in ferocity—usually attempt to avoid out-and-out fighting in their communities. To settle their grievances two enemies may engage in a formal duel in which they take turns, first punching each other in the chest, then slapping each other on the side, and finally, if they have not had enough, clubbing each other on the head. Hopefully, the contest comes to an end before they resort to bloodshed. The Yanomamö have provided carefully graded alternatives to killing.

Violence Must Be Taught To explain the expression of violence, some popular writers insist that aggression, like eye color or blood type, is a genetic trait. Just as spiders spin webs, humans instinctively kick each other around. Aggressive behavior in people is the product of biological inheritance.

There is, however, little evidence that human aggression is the direct result of an inborn pattern. In fact, aside from the infant reaction to falling or loud noise, people are probably instinct-free. Nothing comparable to the inherited nest-building behavior of the South American weaver bird or the inherited honey dance behavior of the bee has been demonstrated in humans.

Not biological impulse but learning and experience largely control the expression of violence in human beings. Like the way people carry a burden or build a shelter, the display of aggression is determined not by inheritance but by education. Within the same human species the anthropologist has no difficulty in identifying both highly aggressive and highly nonaggressive societies. Whether a people are going to embrace murder and treachery or refrain from hurting a chicken depends on their life style. Just as a society may place its stamp of approval on either sexual permissiveness or sexual prudery, so may it accept as appropriate conduct either violence or gentleness.

If the expression of aggression is culturally determined, then it should be affected by social change. The treacherous Kaingang were once a settled peaceful people who were unfortunate enough to live on valuable coffee-producing lands coveted by the Brazilians. Routed from their villages and systematically hunted down by hired gunmen as though they were animals, the survivors fled for their lives into the depths of the forest. Demoralized, fearful of strangers, their family and community structure destroyed, they finally turned on each other, a tranquil people turned into one of the most brutal on earth.

Even the affable Semai, recruited into the British army and trained for jungle warfare, became merciless killers. Yet when they were released from service to resume their old community life, they once again became mild, unaggressive people, exhibiting the kind of conduct their life style demanded of them. Like all other humans, the Semai could be conditioned to express a wide range of behavioral variations.

Why do tribal people fight? The factors that lead humans to kill their own species are many, ranging from population pressure and social and economic inequality to retaliation for past injuries, and fear and jealousy of neighboring communities. In technologically simple socieites, warfare frequently appears where resources are limited and the competition for them is high. Among the ever-feuding Yanomamö, women are in short supply. Since chiefs keep four or five wives, young men must often be without spouses. To resolve their sexual frustration they can arrange affairs with married women—which raises the level of physical conflict within a community—or they can raid enemy villages for women, a practice that quickly leads to counterattacks. Warfare among the Yanomamö appears to stem, at least in part, from their lopsided social arrangements.

Reluctant Warriors Organized warfare is not a universal condition of the human race. The very idea is incomprehensible in some small-scale societies. An Eskimo may murder another man, but the thought of a tribe or nation fighting another! Well, that's just not human. A cannibal chieftain of New Guinea, hearing that European armies sometimes tried to exterminate each other, was incredulous. How could normal people kill more than they could eat!

The amiable Arapesh occasionally get into a brawl with a neighboring village. A band of warriors descends on the enemy settlement and exchanges harsh words. If a warrior in the heat of argument should forget his usual conciliatory manner and hurl a spear, someone on the other side may hurl a spear back, not to kill the thrower but to shake him up a bit. If anyone does get hurt, the attacking party promptly runs off. The Arapesh, even under provocation, cannot bring themselves to warfare. There are a good many societies like the Arapesh. A study of four hundred cultures around the world reveals that less than one quarter of them can be described as warlike.

The Maring of New Guinea are a savage and bellicose people. Yet some of their conflicts look like medieval tournaments rather than out-and-out battles. Incited by their war wizards the combatants dance toward the enemy, singing, stamping their feet, and crying "Oooooo." Arriving at the field of action both sides set their shields into the earth. The battle formally gets under way when a warrior leaves the protection of his shield to shout taunts at the opposing side, who then reply with a hail of arrows. But the battle promptly comes to an end with the first death. At that point a truce is declared which gives the warriors an excuse for returning home to engage in elaborate and prolonged funeral rites.

The nineteenth-century Crow Indians of the American Plains were bold, tough fighters feared by all their neighbors. Yet their military ideal was not the destruction of the enemy but counting coup, a fighting game which brought honor not so much for a killing as for a stunt. A coup (a blow directed against an enemy) could be any one of four deeds: Number one, meriting the greatest glory, consisted of touching an enemy in battle and, without killing him, getting away unscathed. Snatching a bow or gun from an enemy in a hand-to-hand encounter ranked second. Theft of an enemy's picketed horse was third. Leadership of a raid was the last honor. It took far more skill and courage, from the Crow point of view, to touch an enemy than to kill him from a distance with a weapon. Unfortunately for the Crow, their passion for turning warfare into a game worked in the Indian wars to the advantage of the federal troops who had no scruples about killing from a distance. The Americans gloried in counting not coup but bodies.

It may come as a surprise that tribal warriors often have little zest for fighting. The Yanomamö train their children from their early years to be fighters. Parents may compel their eight-year-old sons to beat each other up. As the boys grow older, they take hallucinogenic drugs, in part to maintain their fighting spirit. Yet when the Yanomamö go off on a raid, the closer they draw to the battlefield, the less their enthusiasm for the conflict sometimes grows. Long before they sight the enemy, some of the fierce fighters have turned home, complaining of painful backs, sore legs, or stomachache. Despite their great capacity for rage, the Yanomamö may make reluctant warriors.

Soldiers in contemporary Western nations display a similar hesitancy about fighting. Modern armies in time of war could never fulfil their quotas without a compulsory service system. Notwithstanding the pressure of public opinion and enlistment promises to learn a trade or see the world, young people usually must be drafted into the armed forces of their country. Many soldiers have deserted even before they engage in battle. Soldiers confronting the enemy frequently must be driven forward by the pistols and swords of their officers. Some of the great battles of modern times have been fought by armies that were roaring drunk. If humans have a gene programmed for violence it often seems to propel them away from rather than toward the slaughter.

For those who feel impelled to work off violent impulses civilized warfare can be very frustrating. The use of long-range weaponry makes it difficult to feel aggressive toward an enemy who cannot be seen. In an era of push-button warfare the release of a bomb can be as impersonal as punching the keys of an office computer. Caught in the dreary routine of a modern conflict, soldiers are dominated not by an innate drive to commit acts of violence, but by fear, boredom, homesickness, and sexual frustration. War is not in our genes but in our culture.

Legitimizing Violence Though contrary to biological and anthropological evidence, the doctrine of innate human aggression persists as an explanation of such problems as the increasing crime rate, racial conflict, international terrorism, traffic accidents, school vandalism, and wars large and small. It is far easier to conclude that the expression of violence is natural to humanity than to ferret out its causes in the social and economic complexities of our society. After all, we cannot be held responsible for what we have inherited. By clinging to the idea that human beings are naturally aggressive we can rid ourselves of our own guilt and at the same time legitimize our violence whether in war or peace.

We return to the Milgrim experiment. No generation of Americans has ever been exposed to a greater display of daily violence. Propped on his cushion, the television viewer can tune in on a variety of wars, plane disasters, highway accidents, gangland shoot-outs, racial conflict, and other mayhem, real and fictional. American children learn to accept the presence of brutality on the screen, as Yanomamö youngsters learn to live with it in their daily life. It has been estimated that by the age of thirteen the average American child has witnessed eight thousand TV murders. Many playthings are in the form of daggers, machine guns, tanks, rockets, and nuclear bombs. A toothbrush for use in the nursery is shaped like a derringer.

A new coin-operated game called "Death Race" that puts players behind the wheel trying to run down humanoid figures on a television screen is apparently catching on in amusement parks around the country. . . . For a quarter, a player gets a minute to chase and run down all the symbolic pedestrians he can. Hitting one of the figures rewards the player with an electronic shriek and points scored on a grave marker. . . . The National Safety Council describes "Death Race" as . . . "sick, sick, sick."

—New York Times, *1976*

There has been a great deal of controversy about the interpretation of the Milgrim experiment. We surmise that long before the volunteers entered the laboratory at Yale, they had been conditioned to tolerate violence as an inevitable aspect of contemporary living. Passive viewers, they were quite unaware of how easily they could be pushed into becoming active participants in a cruel exercise.

Some of the subjects in the experiment were undoubtedly seduced by what they perceived as the "higher" authority of a great university that could do no wrong. Others may have considered the alleged scientific purpose of the experiment and convinced themselves that they were advancing the cause of human knowledge. (When the experiment was repeated later under the auspices of an organization without any university affiliation, the results were not very different.) And it seems that a substantial number of the volunteers did as they were told because it was easier to continue than to say No and get up and walk out. Urged on by a stranger, a housewife who would not have harmed a pussycat was willing to throw the switches that apparently caused a fellow human to scream in agony.

Whether a person will reach for the 450-volt switch or not depends in part on his values, that is, his standards of what is desirable or undesirable conduct. We turn to the values people live by and again begin with an invented situation.

the values people live by

10

"The Sound of Your Hammer at Five in the Morning"

A THIRD-YEAR student at the Princeton Theological Seminary hurriedly approaches the broadcasting studio where he is scheduled to deliver a sermon on the parable of "The Good Samaritan"* At the entrance of the studio a stranger is lying on the ground, but the student has been cautioned to appear on time and rushes by. Fifteen minutes later a second student who has received the same assignment comes to the door. The man is still lying on the ground, and he is groaning now. Immersed in his own thoughts, the student does not notice the stranger and hurries up to the studio. Sometime later a third student appears. The man has shifted his position so that his body now blocks the entrance. The student steps over him and rushes upstairs. In the course of the day the remaining members of the class appear at intervals to deliver their sermon. All encounter

*A certain man went down from Jerusalem to Jericho and fell among thieves which stripped him of his raiment and wounded him and departed, leaving him half dead. . . a certain Samaritan, as he journeyed, came where he was, and when he saw him, he had compassion on him and bound up his wounds, pouring in oil and wine and set him on his own beast, and brought him to an inn and took care of him. . . .—Luke, 10:30–37

the man on the ground. Most ignore him. To those who stop to inquire if they can be of any help, the stranger replies vaguely, quickly gets to his feet, and walks off without any difficulty.

The whole situation was a deception, including the assignment of the sermon, the instruction to appear exactly on time, and the apparent distress of the stranger at the door. A camera hidden in a window across the street had recorded the students' encounter with the stranger. All the students had been taught that they were their brother's keeper. Yet in a crucial situation most forgot this fundamental value. According to the sociologists who structured this experiment, the students were confronted with conflicting values. Had they stopped to help the stranger they would have been late for their assignment. Punctuality is also an American value.

What Is a Value? Values are standards of personal and social conduct about which people have strong feelings, sometimes so strong that they may be ready to kill or be killed for them. Values—such as patriotism, honesty, justice, generosity, or personal cleanliness—refer not to what a person actually does or wishes to do, but to what he *ought* to do. The mother who cries out in exasperation, "And don't forget to use soap this time," is expressing a value of her culture.

What is desirable, fitting, or good may vary widely from society to society. Work is a great virtue for Americans. A person who stays away from the office for a day hastens to explain himself to his neighbors. A Xingu Indian, however, feels no shame when his relatives come upon him smoking and exchanging stories on the bench in front of the men's house instead of clearing his garden. For him "time-off" is no offence.

The Nyakyusa of Tanzania in eastern Africa stress a virtue they call *ukwangala,* or the enjoyment of good company. A boy brings home a large company of friends. The father smiles proudly when his wives complain that the boy and his friends have consumed all the milk and bananas in the house. "You say he entertained six friends. Ah, that son of mine is going to be a great chief someday." Sociability is a prime Nyakyusa value.

On the island of Dobu, off the coast of New Guinea, sociability is viewed with intense suspicion. "If we wish to kill a man," a Dobuan once said, "we eat, sleep, work, and rest with him for several months. We flatter him, smile on him, and bide our time. Then when his guard is down we invite him to our house and feed him a poisoned meal." Always fearful of treachery, the Dobuans must warn their children of the perils of sociability. The values cherished by one people may be feared by another.

Acquiring and Sharing People in industrial states place high value on material well-being and the acquisition of possessions. Many measure their success in terms of their bank balance, the size of their home, the kind of car they drive, or the number of gadgets in their rumpus room. The good life depends on attaining an ever higher standard of material living.

Other societies view material wealth with intense suspicion. In many small-scale communities people often seem to have a veritable terror of amassing possessions. They burn, bury, or distribute them at feasts and funerals. When a Kaingang Indian receives a gift, he gives it away. When he dies, his worldly goods are destroyed—even his precious dogs.

Status in small tribal groups frequently depends on what one gives away. A mountain Arapesh hunter doesn't eat the game he has killed but turns it over to a relative. A man who would consume his own kill, even if it were only a tiny bird, would be a contemptible creature. "Food withheld will be your death. See whoever enters your home obtains something to eat," the Winnebago Indians of Wisconsin used to say. The Plains Indians despised hoarders intensely and greatly respected fellow tribesmen who freely parted with food, arrows, hides, and even horses—giving them to guests and destitute neighbors. Handouts were an expression of dearly held values.

Willingness to give up possessions or share food doesn't

mean that people in small-scale communities are saints. In many simple societies, sharing helps survival when the going is rough. The fisherman who distributes part of his catch among his neighbors today will eat tomorrow although he comes home with an empty creel. As people in industrial societies save money for a rainy day, other cultures store reserves of goodwill. Sharing provides people with the advantages of a social security system.

The Indians are so free with all they possess that no one would believe it without having seen it. Of anything you wish if you ask them for it they never say No. Rather they invite the person to share it and show as much love as though they were giving their hearts.

—Christopher Columbus, 1492

The Work Ethic Simple and complex societies often differ in their attitudes toward work. If anything riles the older generation in America, it is the behavior of young people who do not hold a regular nine-to-five job, but spend their time skiing, surfing, backpacking, or playing tennis. The school truant is understandable, the work truant detestable.

The sound of your hammer at five in the morning or at eight at night heard by a creditor makes him easy six months longer; but if he sees you at a billiard table or hears your voice at a tavern when you should be at work, he sends for his money the next day.

—Benjamin Franklin

Work is far more than an economic necessity in the industrial state. It is a moral obligation, a social duty, and a mark of status. Let strangers meet and one of the first questions is, "What kind of work do you do?" A child hardly out of kindergarten is asked what she is going to do when she grows up. An unemployed adult feels lost and unwanted.

In small-scale communities work is often regarded far more casually. The Arunta, who live in one of the most inhospitable regions on earth, are among the world's most leisured people.

Industrial societies generally draw a neat line between work and leisure activities. The floor plan of a supermarket is designed to discourage everything but shopping. A tribal market, on the other hand, can easily turn into a festival. People come not only to buy and sell but also to meet friends; gossip; pass the news of the day; watch jugglers, dancers, and magicians; or just have a good time. Work mixes casually with social life. • The town market at Bamako, Mali, West Africa.

When wild food is available they hunt and gather with undiminished vigor, but they stop short as soon as they have met their immediate needs and give themselves over to feasting, visiting, and ceremonials. Without means of storage of what use would it be to gather food that would soon spoil? Besides, steady work would quickly become counterproductive. A band that kept itself busy eight hours a day every day in the week would dangerously reduce the supply of game and wild plants and thereby do perhaps irreversible damage to the environment.

People in simple societies often mingle work and play. Erecting a new house, launching a canoe, rounding up game, or netting fish may be accompanied by singing, dancing, dramatics, or horseplay. Industrial workers, on the other hand, do no dancing on the factory floor. In technologically advanced societies the areas of work and play are sharply separated. Work is serious; play is frivolous and is to be undertaken only when the significant economic responsibilities of the day or week have been accomplished. In pre-industrial America combining work and play was characteristic of frontier and farming life. Our vast repertory of work songs and dances reminds us of a time when barn raisings, threshing parties, and harvest festivals provided the occasion both for fun and hard labor.

In recent years the view that work is an ultimate value has come under increasing challenge in America. The worker on the modern assembly line feels little sense of fulfillment. Unlike the tribal craftsman who molds a pot, fashions a harpoon, or designs a mask, he derives little or no emotional satisfaction from his job. At the end of the day's work he may hurry home to a hobby which gives him the feeling of accomplishment his employment has failed to provide.

> Climbing taxes you both physically and mentally and makes maximum use of your body and mind. . . . When I climb I really feel alive.
>
> —*George Willig, the young American who ascended the face of the 102-story World Trade Center in New York*

Many people seek creativity and spontaneity away from the job in games, sport, travel, or music. What they do after working hours is more significant than what they do at their job, trade, or profession. Social status has begun to depend not only on what people do when they are working but on what they do when they are not working. In the last decades of the twentieth century the pursuit of leisure activities has become a respected American goal.

Cooperation and Competition Small-scale societies will generally place greater stress on cooperation than on competition in their scale of values. Among the Eskimos cooperation is an essential virtue which helps them survive in a harsh environ-

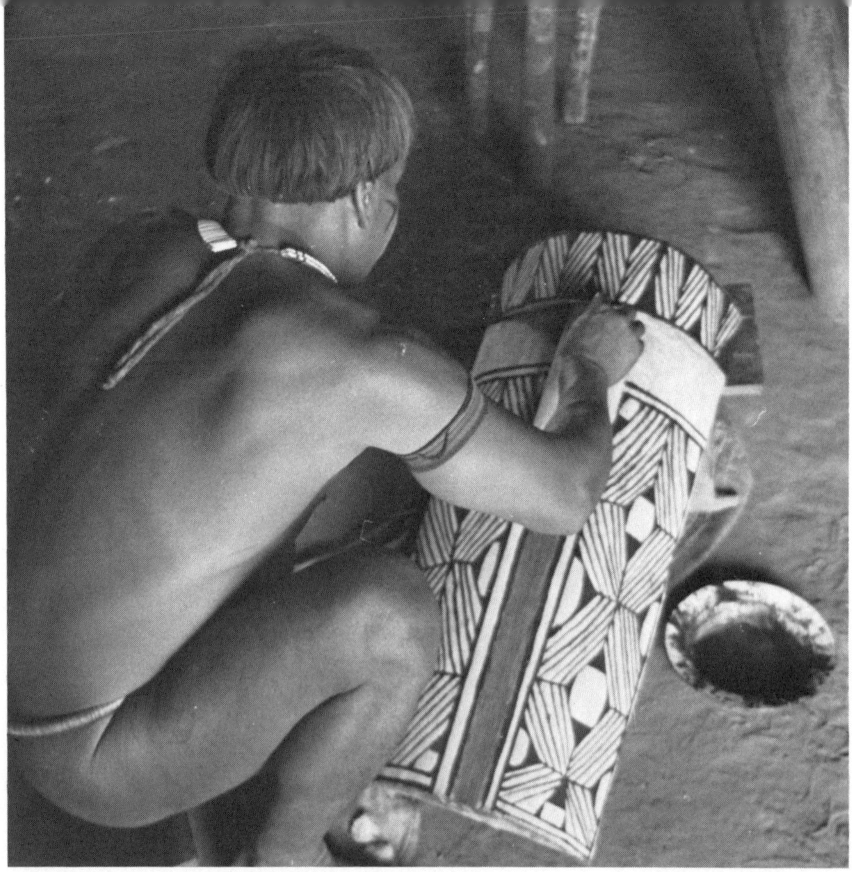

An industrial worker is usually governed by the impersonal rhythm of the machine he tends. Working for a certain number of hours rather than to accomplish a specific task, he rarely experiences the satisfaction of seeing the end result of his labors. The pre-industrial worker is a craftsman who can derive deep pleasure from his work. • In an Indian village along the Xingu River in central Brazil, an artist carves a ceremonial mask.

ment. Men hunt together and share their catch. Women assist each other with household responsibilities. Related families use the same equipment and join in repairing each other's houses. Still the Eskimos are a competitive people. They love sports such as running, dog-team races, and story and song contests. Women compete in sewing skins and making baskets, men in building kayaks and fashioning harpoons. Rivalry, though encouraged, is expected to be good-natured. A person must never boast or flaunt his skills. Returning from a successful hunt, a hunter will say, "Oh, anybody could have done that."

The Hopi disapprove of any kind of competition. They will never play a game in which score is kept. To get ahead of others is shameful. At work a Hopi enjoys cooperative enterprises such as sheep shearing or crop gathering, but not activities in which individual effort is noticeable. When he works for the white man he tries to avoid becoming foreman, preferring the same wages as his fellows. Among the neighboring Zuni Indians, people dislike being singled out so much that when a priestly post has to be filled all the qualified males must be confined behind locked doors until one of them capitulates and accepts the office.

Some small-scale societies, on the other hand, honor individual ambition, self-assertion, and getting ahead of others. The Kwakiutl Indians (whose marriage customs allowed them to marry the limbs of a title holder) competed with each other in vast feasts called *potlatches.* Two chiefs would try to outdo each other in the amount of property they could give away or destroy. To best his rival a chief might burn vast quantities of furs and blankets, destroy great war canoes, and even kill his own slaves. To save himself from lifetime disgrace his opponent would then have to destroy an equal amount of wealth. "We do not fight with weapons," said the Kwakiutl. "We fight with property."

In the light of Kwakiutl history the custom is not as mad as it may seem. Formerly the potlatch, like the feasts of other small-scale societies, had been an occasion in which a chief gained prestige by giving away his surplus food and possessions. The potlatch acted as a leveling device and prevented the accumulation of wealth by a few. But after the arrival of the Europeans in the Canadian Northwest, the chiefs became immensely wealthy in the fur trade. At the same time the Indian population, because of the introduction of the white man's diseases, decreased dramatically dropping from 23,000 to 2,000 in a fifty-year period. With more wealth than they could ever consume, the chiefs, in the hope of attracting followers to their dying villages, presented grand spectaculars in which they

Like a heraldic crest or the coat of arms of European nobility, the totem pole that a prominent Pacific Northwest Indian would set up in front of his home proclaimed his rank, title, and achievements. Sometimes the right to the pole was based on the defeat of a rival in a potlatch. The larger the pole, the greater the prestige of the owner. • A totem pole carved by Northwest Coast Indians.

threw their excess property into the flames. Like their totem poles, the potlatch was an advertisment of the power and prestige of the chiefs.

Like people in other industrial societies Americans are highly competitive. Almost from the day that they enter school children are encouraged to get ahead of others. Praise and recognition go to the best speller, the best writer, the best reader, the best runner, or the best artist. Children soon learn that success means surpassing others; failure means being surpassed.

Everybody compares their children. My son Mark was a little slow in getting his first tooth, and with all the talk, I thought I'd go crazy.

—*A young American suburban housewife*

Though unlisted in the course of study, competition is fostered in almost every school in America. With the exception of the Japanese child who, at the age of two or three, is shipped off to a special coaching academy to secure his admission to a prestigious kindergarten, the American student is probably the most harried of young people. Subject to a continuing barrage of personality, intelligence, and achievement tests he is labeled, classified, and channeled throughout his academic career, his sense of self-esteem rising or falling with the level of his scores.

In high school and college the pressure to stay at the head of the class becomes overwhelming so that cheating becomes a way of life for some. To *beat* his classmates a student may sabotage their laboratory experiments or mutilate library references. "Ghosts" manufacture term papers and "ringers" take examinations for both friends and paying clients.

Winning isn't everything; it is the only thing.

—Vince Lombardi, American football coach

Probably no American parent would discourage his son or daughter from competing for a scholarship or an athletic medal. Yet parents in many simple societies who urged their child to come out ahead of others would be violating the most cherished ideals of their culture. Parents on the island of Wogeo say, "Do not compete with your playmate but help him, for if you do he will help you." A passion for getting ahead of others is not a universal human value.

Many simple societies tend to soft-pedal competitiveness if only because status is to a large extent ascribed rather than earned or achieved. You don't have to contend with others for social positions such as that of adult, parent, hunter, farmer, fisherman, elder, or chief. These vital positions are yours by virtue of the fact that you are a member of your family, clan, band, or tribe. This is not to say that people don't know who is the best farmer, hunter, or fisherman, but whether or not you are the best will not affect your social standing or your economic security. Anyone who acquires much more than his neighbors or who boasts of his accomplishments is likely to be brought up short by nasty gossip or, worse, accusations of being a witch.

Industrial societies place great emphasis upon achieved statuses. These are positions that a person earns in life by his own individual effort such as those of graduate student, accountant, factory manager, real estate broker, mayor, and big league ball player. In a world of achieved statuses you get to the top of the ladder by outstripping others. Where social and economic security hinges on individual achievement, getting ahead of others has to be a primary value.

No society, however, could long endure unrestrained competition. Despite the remark of Vince Lombardi, winning is *not* the only thing. Like other societies, America espouses the value of cooperation. Though everyone is expected to struggle for what he gets, he is also expected to wait his turn and queue up, to lend a helping hand, to support his team, to engage in community drives, and to come to the aid of the stranger who lies sprawled on the street. A society may emphasize competiton or cooperation but it must leave room for both in its daily life.

Activism and Fatalism In a small-scale society guided by the traditions of the past, the aged rather than the young will be the most honored members. The upholders of custom and the repositories of wisdom, the elderly provide advice and leadership. Where there are no written records they are a memory bank of knowledge, values, and past history. They are the leaders to whom their juniors respectfully defer. Among wild-food gatherers, however, such as the Eskimos, old people who cannot keep up with the line of march must sometimes be abandoned. In other societies an elder who no longer has young people about him may lose prestige. As the Hopi say, the less one thinks of old age the better off he is.

Technologically advanced states, devoted to change and to the bright promises of the future, value youthfulness over age.

In industrial societies the elderly sometimes feel like useless members of the community. In simple societies the aged, as long as they retain their faculties, are frequently honored for the wisdom supposed to accompany their advancing years and for the special services they contribute, such as storytelling and the performance of magic or priestly duties. In Australian hunting and gathering bands, the rulers were senior citizens, who hazed the young men and monopolized the young women. • An Arunta tribesman from central Australia.

So attractive is the appearance of youthfulness that even the middle-aged often mimic the hair styles, dress, manner, and sexual behavior of the young, sometimes resorting to surgery to obliterate the marks of the years. Grey hairs and wrinkles are a liability for many jobs. Few older women are airline stewardesses. In many occupations compulsory retirement rules force people out of work no matter how capable they may still be. Some must die sociologically before the end of their life span. The accent on youthfulness is deeply ingrained in the values of modern industrial nations.

To live beyond forty is bad taste.

—Feodor Dostoevski, Russian novelist

Americans love youthfulness and the youthful sprit. Refusing to accept things merely because they have been done before, they de-emphasize the past and look forward to the future. Every decade will bring more of the good things of life. Everything is possible; the impossible just takes a little longer.

The new, the modern, and the dynamic are good; the old-fashioned, the antiquated, and the old are bad. Few words are as sacred as *progress*.

My future will bring me all the things I want: a beautiful home, an excellent education for my children, the ability to go when and where I want. We are a people who shine in adversity.

—A twenty-four-year-old American, 1975

The value that underlies belief in progress, competition, youthfulness, hard work, the future, and optimism is *activism*, the doctrine holding that the individual instead of passively accepting the circumstances of his life should actively attempt to change them. Unlike the guru, the hermit, the ascetic, or the philosopher absorbed in inner experience, the American doesn't just sit there, he *does* something. Pledged to action rather than contemplation or renunciation, he conquers space, transforms the environment, changes the weather, smashes the atom, stamps out illiteracy, abolishes poverty.

The doctrine of activism is a reflection of the American experience, an outgrowth of many years of enormous material development and victory over enemies both foreign and domestic. The history of many other peoples, however, has been marked by overwhelming defeat in war and incessant poverty. A Central American peasant who adopted the doctrine of activism would be devoting his life to a hopeless cause. Because of a crude technology and depleted natural resources he would probably end up like his parents no matter how industriously he worked his barren hillside.

Adapting his goals to grim reality he subscribes instead to fatalism, the doctrine declaring that whatever happens will happen, no matter what one does or does not do about it. He has learned to value acceptance and passivity not progress and optimism. No less than other people, he wants to improve his lot in life, but he is wary of false hopes and promises. For him fatalism is an adaptation to the limitations of his way of life.

Recently, some Americans have begun to entertain doubts about their philosophy of activism. They have become aware that many problems may be unsolvable. The application of maximum effort may not always work, nor does technological progress always bring desirable results. People have not become happier or more content because they have accumulated increasing amounts of material goods. The sacred value of the work ethic comes under challenge as millions devote more and more of their time to the pursuit of pleasure.

Leisure is one of America's biggest industries. . . . Between 1965 and 1975, according to the Commerce Department, the nation's cumulative personal expenditures on recreation consumption soared from $25.9 billion to $65.9 billion.

—New York Times, *1977*

The Value of Values Values help people get along with one another. Though all Americans do not think alike, they share a number of common beliefs about what is desirable or undesirable so that they know what they can expect of each other. Our values, for example, tell us that we should hold a regular job, cooperate with fellow workers, take part in community affairs, vote in local and national elections, and offer charity to those in need. The acknowledgment of common values helps a society preserve its unity.

Values are adapted to the life style in which they flourish. The Hopi discouragement of individual ambition and competition serves a society whose survival in a harsh desert environment depends on the closest teamwork. America's emphasis on punctuality makes good sense in an industrial state where airlines, railroads, factories, and other institutions must run on time. In the days when America was founded, the work ethic was as vital to the pioneers as their long rifles. The frontier had no place for the idler or the freeloader.

Every human community operates within the limitations of its available technology and its social and physical environ-

Time is not a great concern to most tribal peoples. In industrial lands time is measured precisely, and punctuality becomes a prized value. To keep the economy functioning workers must arrive at their jobs on time and usually at the same time. • The morning rush hour at the Tokyo Central Station, where 1 million passengers arrive and depart each day. Note that some of the commuters are wearing masks.

ment. The value of sharing food and possessions among the Bushmen of the Kalahari Desert in southern Africa may seem a most attractive virtue. Yet we must remember that reciprocity, or the exchange of valuable goods without calculating how much one has given, is imposed on the Bushmen by the conditions under which they live. The Bushmen are a generous people but unless they subscribed to the value of sharing, they would starve. To survive they can act in no other way.

Can we say that some values are better than others? To us the Zuni reluctance to assume leadership or the Dobuan Islander's fear of sociability may look peculiar. We must, however, be wary about making judgments about the values of other peoples. What we can ask is, "To what extent does a particular value serve the purposes of the society in which it is found? How does a value reinforce, and relate to, other goals in a society?"

Conflict of Values In a complex industrial society people are swayed by a wide and sometimes contradictory range of values. Americans love a winner, yet they often identify with the underdog. Committed to the doctrine that everyone should make his own way in the world, they sympathize with the lowly and the distressed, generously helping victims of war, flood, or earthquake. Fascinated by the new and the untried, they nostalgically collect old furniture, old cars, and old songs.

Conflict between what people ought to do and what they actually do, between the ideal and the actual, is a problem that confronts all cultures. In a Xingu Indian community all the fishermen are expected to share their catch with their neighbors. Still, there are always a few cheats who attempt to sneak into their homes without sharing what they have caught.

Nevertheless, a child who grows up in a small isolated tribal community will probably encounter minimal differences in values. In general, parents, kinfolk, and playmates will subscribe to the same standards of belief and behavior. But in contemporary Western civilization a child need only glance at the television screen to discover a world full of conflicting views of what is right and wrong. The lessons his parents taught are flaunted at almost every twist of the dial. The principles he learns in school of honesty, brotherhood, and patriotism are often ignored by relatives, agemates, and national leaders. In adulthood he comes face to face not with one consistent code but with a broad spectrum of values.

Sometimes divergent values may be reconciled by being restricted to certain times and places. Brotherly love may be the proper reaction among intimate friends, but "minding your own business" may be advisable among strangers on a city street. At Princeton the seminarians were confronted by contradictory demands. Trained to appreciate values such as compassion and cooperation, the majority "scheduled" their humanitarianism for their sermon in the broadcasting studio rather than for the incident in the street. Still, of the forty who unwittingly participated in the experiment, sixteen stopped and tried to help the stranger lying on the ground. In a complex society people can heed the sound of a different drum.*

Everywhere people say that their values have come to them as revelations from the gods, spirits, and ancestors. Let us now look at the nature of religion, which we will define narrowly as belief in supernatural forces together with the behavior which results from such belief.

*The structure of the Princeton experiment, like that of the Milgrim experiment, is a study in value conflict. Both experiments intended to make a contribution to human knowledge, a laudable goal in our society. Yet both experiments depended on gross deception, artfully entrapping people into revealing hidden facets of behavior. Can an institution in an open democratic society ever be justified in making use of fraud and deceit for purposes no matter how worthy?

religion and magic

11

"You Could Not Help but Cry, It Was So Beautiful"

It is late in the evening of November 7, 1973. On the football field of the Astrodome in Houston, Texas, stands a huge seven-level stage of translucent white plastic glowing with light. On the lower levels on upholstered orange chairs sit the members of the family of the young Indian guru Maharaj Ji. Below on the turf are thousands of young people, some cross-legged, others stretched out in trancelike postures, still others standing on their heads or slowly doing Tai Chi exercises. The odor of incense hangs heavy over the field.

The young master appears and ascends to a blue lucite throne at the summit of the stage as two enormous television screens blow up his image. The audience bows in homage; those on the stage climb to the throne and kiss his feet. A stout round-faced teen-aged boy, the master wears a red and gold suit and on his head a miter-shaped crown. He speaks:

"Within a few short years after the cosmic consciousness of all men has been awakened, violence, greed, and hunger will be abolished, the earth will be inhabited by saints, and the

Millennium will be achieved. Until that glorious time all who receive the knowledge from the master will practice meditation and gain happiness without drugs, liquor, meat, or sex."

The master then descends to the field and departs in a flower-garlanded Rolls-Royce.

What Is Religion? The last decades of the twentieth century have been a time of religious ferment in America. Revivals of old faiths have occurred every few years. Some, like that of Maharaj Ji, are apocalyptic and believe, like the Old Testament prophets and the early Christians, that one day the world will suddenly come to an end and be replaced by a better, purer state of existence. Some of these movements are millennial; that is, they promise that the new and glorious era will last one thousand years. Some of the new religions take their inspiration from India, Tibet, and other exotic lands; others, like the Jesus freaks, are offshoots of revivalist sects of frontier America. Some immerse themselves in astrology, witchcraft, demonology, and other forms of the occult. Though often denounced as quackery and superstition by traditional churches, some of these alternative religions number their followers in the hundreds of thousands.

The anthropologist studies religion as he does education, kinship, sexual roles, or other facets of a people's life style. Without considering his own commitments, as though newly arrived from another planet, he concerns himself not with the validity of any doctrine but with its influence on the behavior of those who subscribe to it. He investigates not the existence or nonexistence of gods, angels, ghosts, spirits, or devils but the social consequences of belief in them. The anthropologist does not presume to say that one religion is more valid than another.

Religion is difficult to define. Like the concept of the family, its definition fluctuates with the culture in which it is practiced. Western societies generally maintain a neat line of demarcation between the everyday world of natural events and the supernatural world. Other societies, however, mingle the natural and the supernatural so that all life becomes a religious experience. Among the Navajo the weaver prays at his work. A dream reveals the future. A high wind, addressed by its sacred name, leaves the corn unharmed. A traveler sings a sacred song to keep safe from danger.

When I mention religion, I mean the Christian religion and not only the Christian religion but the Protestant religion and not only the Protestant religion but the Church of England.

—*Parson Thwackum in Henry Fielding's* Tom Jones

If religion is compassionate and if it excludes no one and if it really helps you out in the here and now, that's how you can tell religion—real religion.

—*Stephen Gaskin, leader of The Farm, a Tennessee commune, 1974*

The religious point of view generally holds that our waking senses see only one aspect of reality, the everyday world of normal events. But much that happens—good as well as bad—takes place because there is a hidden side of reality, the supernatural world, which may be favorably or unfavorably disposed toward us. We can come into contact with this hidden aspect of reality and manipulate it in our favor through certain kinds of behavior which may include prayer, sermon, sacrifice, chanting, dancing, or the employment of magic. Religion is more than just belief; it is also a practice or rite, that is, a prescribed ceremonial procedure.

Look here, last week I lit a candle for you and asked you to make my burro well. Early this week I lit another candle for you but my burro is still sick. Well, I'm lighting another candle for you today but mind you it is the last one until my burro gets better.

—*A Mayan Indian prays to his saint*

Magic and Religion Although they both involve the supernatural, there is a distinction in some cultures between magical and religious practices. We are engaged in a religious activity when we call upon a god, saint, spirit, or other supernatural being to cure the sick, quiet a tempest, comfort the distressed, or otherwise disrupt the normal course of events for our sake.

We are engaged in magical activity, on the other hand, when we do not require the intervention of a supernatural being. Instead, we bend nature to our will by means of incantations, spells, charms, and other time-tested techniques. Unlike religious worship which often involves a sense of awe or veneration, magic is frequently precise and matter-of-fact. The possession of the right amulet or talisman, the recitation of an appropriate incantation, or the stabbing of a doll restores health, stops a thief, or fatally injures an enemy. Using directions like those found in a machine shop manual, magic becomes a form of supernatural mechanics that could appeal to anyone who has ever assembled a bike or radio set from a knockdown kit.

> Don't return a knife in any way but the way it was given, open or closed.
> Serve beef stew on board and it will bring a gale.
> Whistle and you whistle up a breeze
>
> —*New England fishermen's magic lore*

While religion often involves itself with the ultimate problems of human existence, magic keeps busy attempting to achieve immediate and practical results—improving the chances of the fisherman, the hunter, the pregnant woman, or the anxious lover. To help his wife deliver her baby, a Hopi husband rubs her down with the skin of a weasel, so that the infant will emerge into the world with as much ease as the animal slips through a hole.

Magic may serve both good and bad purposes. In some societies sorcerers who are specialists in the use of medicines and other objects for inflicting harm may be hired to dispense illness and even death. Witches are fellow workers in black magic, but unlike sorcerers they never operate in the open. They require no special apparatus because their evil thoughts suffice.

In some tribal communities witchcraft is used to explain events that Western peoples attribute to chance or bad luck. Suppose several children are playing under a granary. The structure falls, and the children are injured. Everyone knows that the granary has been weakened by termites. But why did it collapse precisely at the moment that the children ran under it? "Witchcraft," say the Azande people of central Africa. There must be a witch in the village who is responsible for the deed. Witchcraft explains the unexplainable.

In recent years many Westerners have become fascinated by the occult, that is, the knowledge and use of secret and mysterious agencies such as witchcraft, magic, astrology, faith healing, tarot card reading, and various forms of mysticism. Practices and beliefs once associated with the Dark Ages and "uncivilized" peoples have become both popular and respectable, a development that should not surprise us for religion and magic have always overlapped. Religious pictures, holy relics, sacred books, and medals in almost all faiths have long been believed to heal, avert evil, or bring prosperity. The magic devotee and the religious believer may be the same person, who earnestly attends church on Sunday to invoke divine guidance and avidly consults the astrology column of his newspaper on Monday to discover what lies ahead for him during the week.

Religion is Adaptive No society, no matter how simple its technology, and no people, no matter how intense their commitment to science, are without faith in the supernatural. No less than the Middle Ages or ancient times, the twentieth century provides a fruitful climate for religion. When we consider how universal religion is we may conclude that it is adaptive, conferring substantial benefits upon its followers.

We live in perpetual suspense between life and death, plenty and want, which are distributed among the human species by secret and unknown causes whose operation is oft unexpected and always unaccountable.

—*David Hume, Scottish philosopher, 1757*

Everywhere religion suggests answers to life's mysteries. Like an architect's blueprint, it provides an orderly profile of the scheme of things and conveys a sense of security even in the face of circumstances beyond individual or community control. Despite the tremendous resources of the most advanced technological society, humans are never fully in command. Religious myths present solutions to life's deepest mysteries. "In the beginning God created heaven and earth" tells Western peoples how the universe came to be. An Australian myth explains life and death: Babies enter their mother's womb in the form of the food she eats; a dream announces to the father that he is about to have a child. At death a person returns to a spirit house, where in a "state of plenty" he awaits his next time around to be born.

Among tribal peoples myths are also codes of morals and manners which tell people how and why they are to behave. Asked why women sit in a particular way, the Navajo reply, "Because the Holy People did it that way." Their children, asked why they play a game according to certain rules, give the same response. Myths lend authority to social custom.

No society has yet eliminated the element of uncertainty in human life. A person makes a halfhearted effort and succeeds. He does his utmost and fails. Few hunters are as knowledgeable and skilled as the Eskimos and yet they often cannot predict what will happen. A hunter has barely left his home before he runs down and kills a seal. A week later all the game has vanished. What recourse does he have? The next time he kills a seal he presents it with a drink of water for, if he placates its soul, game will remain plentiful in his neighborhood. Where people have little control over a situation, they may implement their efforts with an appeal to the supernatural. Few willingly go it alone.

People are not likely to call on the supernatural for help when they are certain of the outcome. Central Caroline Islanders in the western Pacific, for example, would not think of employing magic to help their breadfruit trees grow. They have never had a crop failure. But they use lots of magic when they embark on a long and uncertain canoe voyage over the ocean. Together with other sea-going people they bank on the supernatural in dangerous, unpredictable situations.

In proportion as any man's life is governed by accident, he increases in superstition, as may be particularly observed of gamesters and sailors.

—*David Hume, 1757*

In America baseball players together with racing car drivers, test pilots, sky divers, and lovers are notoriously given to superstition. (Superstitions are beliefs in the supernatural that we don't happen to share. One person's sacred ritual is another's nonsense.) In a baseball game once the ball leaves the hand of the pitcher, the outcome cannot be predicted. He may throw his best curve ball and see it go sailing over the fence for a grand slam. By any number of magical acts—tugging at his cap, smoothing the dirt around the mound, or touching the resin bag—a pitcher seeks to conquer the element of uncertainty in the game.

Hitters too engage in superstitious practices for hitting is a chancey affair, luck playing a large part in determining whether the ball will plunk right into a waiting glove or fly down the base line for a scorching two bagger. A big league player, George Gmelch, said that, hoping to maintain a batting streak, he once "ate fried chicken every day at four P.M., kept my eyes closed during the National Anthem, and changed sweat shirts at the end of the fourth inning seven consecutive nights—until the streak ended."

Religion gives people confidence that they can cope with an unpredictable situation; it also gives them a feeling of social solidarity. An Australian band is held together by the belief that every member is descended from the same sacred spirit. Moslems, when they bow toward Mecca in their daily devotions, experience a sense of unity though they may be citizens of countries as far removed as Egypt and the Philippines. In America young people in search of companionship and an outlet for their youthful idealism turn to sects whose alien rituals help to bind them together. The greater the public resentment or the cries of outraged parents, the more the believers cling to a shared body of creed and rite. Outside antagonism strengthens their sense of common fellowship.

An entire society may be held together by its religion. No chief or council wields firm authority in a Hopi village. Nevertheless, the kin or family groups that make up the community cooperate under the leadership of religious organizations that engage in an annual cycle of ceremonies intended to bring the life-giving rain to the village. Other societies may be organized on the basis of politics, trade, or defense. The Hopis are organized on the basis of religious ceremonial.

Emile Durkheim, the French sociologist, was fascinated by the unifying power of religion and conceived of it as a social construct symbolizing all that a people consider sacred.* What was most sacred in any society, he thought, was the society itself. Like the gods, society is something outside the individual. Like the gods, society is immortal, and, again like the gods, society overshadows the thoughts and actions of its members. A society is to its people as a god is to his worshippers. If we must look for a source of religion, we should find it in society and in the needs of society.

If religion does play a unifying role in society, then we would expect supreme deities to appear in communities where

*Durkheim distinguished between the profane and the sacred. For him the profane was the sphere of the ordinary, the familiar, and the taken-for-granted. The sacred was the sphere of the extraordinary, beyond the commonplace and the expected. The sacred includes not only the supernatural but rites we usually do not associate with religion such as the salute to the flag, observance of national holidays, school commencements, weddings.

Shrines, monuments, churches, and temples are outward expressions of the power of a religion to promote and maintain the social order and bind the community together. • A stupa, or temple commemorating the life of Buddha, in Nepal.

there were rich and poor, the powerful and the weak, nobility and commoners, and classes and castes; that is, in societies in which inequality might tear the social order apart unless there were a powerful supernatural authority to support the authority of the king and his nobility. And so it seems to be. Belief in a supreme god, or gods, occurs most frequently not in small-scale simple societies but in complex states in which there are strong inequalities of wealth, social position, rank, and land holding.

As an expression of social solidarity religion can be a conservative force, the principal prop of privilege and tradition. The gods of ancient Rome, ancient Egypt, and the western Pacific generally aligned themselves on the side of the existing order, reinforcing the rule of the monarch or the domination of the ruling class. In India the poverty and suffering of the lower castes has been justified by the religious doctrine of karma, according to which a person is born many times. Good deeds may help to propel him into a higher caste in the next life but do not affect his present status. Rather than protest his lot in this life he patiently awaits his destiny in the next. Heavenly command maintains social inequality.

However, we should not expect to trace religion to a single source. Although religion has often been the spiritual bulwark of the misrule of kings and princes, it can also express the highest aspirations of humanity. Sometimes it arises from the insatiable curiosity of people to delve behind the inscrutable face of the universe and find the answers to the problems of life and death. In times of uncertainty and misfortune religion provides relief from fear and anxiety, helping people adjust to the stresses and difficulties of daily existence.

Revitalization Though religion is said to be founded on divine revelation and unalterable truth, it is like all other cultural institutions subject to change, especially under strong social and economic pressure. A religion may be profoundly altered to meet the threat of internal disruption or outside dangers. Demoralized by the shattering of their culture, an oppressed people may turn to a mystical leader or messiah for help in what is called a revitalization or messianic movement. On the islands of Melanesia in the western Pacific where the inhabitants have lost their lands to the invading whites, revitalization is associated with Cargo cults. A leader appears who announces that he has had a vision telling him that planes carrying a great cargo will soon arrive loaded with everything the people need. Hunger will be abolished, lands recovered, the white man stripped of this power. The dead will return and be reunited with their relatives. There will come a new age in which death, poverty, and old age will be unknown. Captivated by the new doctrine the people erect radio antennae made of bamboo, cut an airstrip through the jungle, and await the arrival of the miraculous planes. But though they wait neither the cargo nor the new age ever comes.

Revitalization movements arose among some of the Indian tribes in America almost every time they suffered disastrous defeat at the hands of the white invaders. The Ghost Dance, the most famous of these movements, got under way about the time that the buffalo upon which the tribes of the western Plains relied for food were killed off. A number of Indian prophets announced that the dead would soon return from the spirit world together with the bison. To bring about this happy day the Indians were told to dance attired in special ghost shirts which would make them invulnerable to the white man's bullets. But the Ghost Dance cult slowly died out, shattered by the federal massacre of more than two hundred Sioux men, women, and children on December 29, 1890, at Pine Ridge, South Dakota.

Once hope of resistance faded, Indian revitalization took a passive stand. Instead of stirring up visions of the return of the buffalo and the disappearance of the white man, new religions such as the Native American Indian Church called upon the Indians to achieve moral perfection and self-knowledge, sometimes with the help of peyote, a narcotic made from the mescaline cactus, and other hallucinogenic drugs.

> I hear something . . . a sound . . . a kind of ring . . . like a star . . . it comes real close right up in front of me . . . just like one of them fireworks . . . I could see everything clear. . . . It was a message from Heaven. I was doing the right thing.
>
> —*An Indian peyote worshipper*

Members of the Native American Indian Church follow Peyote Road, an ethical creed that demands from its followers self-reliance, brotherly love, and avoidance of alcohol. With the help of visions brought on by eating peyote, the worshippers confess their sins and resolve to follow a better way of life. This religion has spread, creating a sense of solidarity among tribes who were formerly enemies. A syncretic creed, it merges elements of Christianity with such traits of Indian cultures as visions.

Revitalization movements have something in common with the new cults that have attracted young people in America. All

Communication with the supernatural may be sought by singing, dancing, spirit possession, praying, sacrifice, drug taking, self-mutilation, meditation, and other acts that attempt to take the worshipper beyond the limits of everyday existence. • Japanese monks at zazen, *or meditation, sit in a cross-legged posture.*

have arisen in periods of rapid change and social stress when many begin to doubt the truth of old values. All center on a magnetic leader who promises his followers a bright future whether they are conquered Indian tribes, subjugated Pacific Islanders, or young people in contemporary America. Revitalization is the religion of the oppressed.

Experiencing the Supernatural In small-scale societies religious rituals generally encourage self-expression and emotional release in order to communicate with the supernatural. By such means as singing, dancing, drugs, self-deprivation, or torture, worshippers attempt to transcend ordinary experience and attain the world of the spirit. The Cora Indians of Mexico spin about in a dance that leaves them in an ecstatic trancelike state. The whirling dervishes, a Moslem brotherhood in the Middle East, commune with the supernatural in a similar fashion. Members of another dervish order in Iraq force steel skewers through their cheeks, apparently without shedding blood, to achieve an out-of-body state. The Indians of the American Plains tried to penetrate the barriers of the supernatural by means of fasting and self-torture. To obtain a vision a Cheyenne allowed himself to be tied to a pole with wooden pins driven through his flesh, tormenting himself by walking back and forth until he had torn himself free.

Some religions emphasize individual contact with the spirit world. The young Crow Indian went into the wilderness alone to find his vision. Other religions stress the role of an intermediary, such as a priest or shaman, who intervenes with the supernatural in behalf of believers. The priest is a full-time specialist usually found in complex societies who receives his authority from his religious denomination. The shaman, on the other hand, works part-time in small-scale societies and is said to acquire his power through natural gifts or his own efforts.

> We do not believe in any god as you do. . . . We do not understand the hidden things but we do believe the people who say they do. We believe our *angakok*, our magician, and we believe him because we wish to live long and because we do not wish to die of famine and starvation. . . . If we did not believe the magician the animals we hunt would make themselves invisible to us.
>
> —*A Polar Eskimo*

Called a medicine man among North American Indians, a witch doctor in Africa, and an *angakok* among the Eskimos, the shaman locates game for hunters, finds lost objects, heals the sick, and drives demons from the bodies of the possessed. A Siberian shaman begins a healing session by singing, dancing, and beating on his tambourine until he becomes invulnerable to pain and falls into a trance, during which he journeys into the spirit world. On his return, supplied with medical advice given by the spirits, he diagnoses his patient's illness and prescribes remedies.

Among the Tapirapé Indians of Brazil, the shaman "eats smoke," swallowing great gulps of tobacco smoke from his

Male or female part-time religious specialists are known as witch doctors in Africa, angakoks *among the Eskimo, shamans in the Arctic and South America, and medicine men in North America. They perform such functions as healing the sick, warding off evil spirits, predicting the future, locating game and lost objects, and generally giving people the confidence to cope with difficult situations. • Women witch doctors dance in a village in Dahomey, West Africa.*

pipe. He sucks at various places on the body of his patient and then vomits large quantities of material from his stomach as evidence that he has removed the offending illness from the sick person.

The Charismatic Movement In America at the present time there is an increasing trend toward self-expression and spontaneous devotion in religious worship. Dissatisfied with formal services such as sermons, believers seek a more direct means of communication with the supernatural. One form of worship that is rapidly growing in even the conventional churches is the renewal of the Pentecostal or charismatic movement that flourished in the United States in the South and West one hundred years ago.

Pentecostal worship stresses the charisms, or spiritual gifts, mentioned in the New Testament. These include healing; prophecy; exorcism, or the casting out of evil spirits; and glossolalia, or speaking in strange tongues.

There appeared to them [the twelve apostles of Christ] tongues of fire . . . resting on each one of them. And they were filled with the Holy Spirit and began to speak in other tongues as the spirit gave them utterance.

—*Acts 2:4*

Like nineteenth-century revivalism, Pentecostal worship is marked by the unabashed display of deep emotion. People are free to let the spirit seize them as it will and then speak in tongues. Though the utterances bear no relation to any known language, the speakers feel a vast sense of peace and happiness.

"Ye ked ee akay kan daee shangda": the sound came out as though I had known how to do it all my life. It was so natural and beautiful. I felt a great peace and happiness. And I cried, you could not help but cry. It was so beautiful.

—*An American Pentecostal worshipper, 1975*

Sometimes in the course of a service people who believe they are possessed by demons may fall into a trancelike state. The minister addresses the demon by name and demands that it leave the possessed person. The demon replies and usually reluctantly obeys. The worshipper then awakens as though from sleep, refreshed and relieved.

Though it may be outside the mainstream, Pentecostal worship has long been part of the American religious tradition. The exotic cults, however, that have recently become so popular in the United States seemed completely beyond the prevailing culture when they appeared in the 1960s. What had America to do with incense burning, cross-legged meditation, Zen, Tai Chi, mantras, star readings, or demonology? Apparently opposed to the scientific direction of the greatest technological state on earth, these cults nevertheless attracted increasing numbers of adherents. Generally youth oriented, appealing principally to young people from the ages of eighteen to twenty-four, they helped to spark a revival of interest in

Confronted with misfortune and death, people everywhere turn to magic and religion to help cope with their anxiety. • Worshippers praying in the Badhshahi Mosque, Lahore, Pakistan.

religion. Together with the trend toward more personal expression in traditional worship, these movements seemed to signify a deeper longing for meaning in life than had been satisfied by the accumulation of possessions, competitiveness, or material success.

Whether in a tribal community or in a modern industrial state, humans everywhere acknowledge by belief and behavior the existence of forces and beings other than those encountered in everyday existence. By whatever name they give it and sometimes by no name at all, people feel an overriding need to communicate with and manipulate the supernatural. In America religious behavior continues to demonstrate itself in a vast variety of activities ranging from rites of passage for birth, marriage, and death to Bible readings, superstitious practices, church attendance, and the ready welcome offered to new creeds.

Almost everywhere demons, spirits, and gods mimic the social and personal lives of their followers, speaking the same language, eating the same food, and expressing hostility, sorrow, or pleasure in much the same fashion. The gods apparently share culture with mortals. We now examine the nature of culture, beginning with the discovery of a wild boy named Victor.

culture and culture change

12

"God Gave to Every People a Cup and from the Cup They Drank Their Life"

IN 1799, a few years after the French Revolution, a boy of about twelve was captured by hunters in the woods of Aveyron in southwestern France. Without clothing and unable to speak a single word or understand what was said to him, he had apparently been living alone in the wilderness for many years. The sensational news of the child's discovery aroused the intense interest of the scientists and educators of the day. If in truth this young "savage" had been living in isolation cut off from all human contact, here was a grand opportunity to discover what part society and what part nature played in the development of language and intelligence by giving him the training he had never acquired.

Accordingly, the boy was dispatched to Paris and placed in the custody of a young physician, Jean-Marc-Gaspard Itard. Taking the boy, whom he named Victor, into his own home, Dr. Itard patiently and gently attempted to give him the skills and experiences he had never gained. The project was only a partial success for although the boy learned to understand much of what was said to him and to eat, sleep, and keep him-

Humans are naked animals who possess neither the brute strength of the water buffalo, the tusks of the elephant, nor the claws of the lion. People would have perished from the earth without the aid of culture, which enables them to cope with the physical environment. • Left, an Australian tribesman starts a fire by twirling a stick against a piece of wood. Right, an Ifugao tribesman in the Philippines looks over the rice terraces of his people. These terraces are at least three thousand years old.

self clean like other twelve-year-olds, he never learned to utter more than a word or two. Was Victor feebleminded? Or had Victor been damaged so badly, emotionally and mentally, by his isolation during the most impressionable time of his life that no training, no matter how conscientious, could restore his full faculties? We will never know, for after a few years Dr. Itard abandoned Victor's reeducation.

What Makes Us Human? What makes the story of Victor so fascinating, although inconclusive, is that he was the core of an experiment no scientist would ever dare attempt: taking a child at an early age and rearing him in isolation. We would imagine that such a child removed from its mother at birth and brought up in a mechanical setting where it would never hear or see another person would be unable to speak or understand speech. Sounds would be mere background noise. Victor at first paid no attention to the sound of a door opening, a dinner bell, or a gunshot so that people thought he was deaf. Objects as simple as a chair would be meaningless. We see a chair as a chair only because people about us treat it as a chair. We learn meanings through contact with other people. Accustomed to the company of other humans, we are unaware of the decisive role they play in our learning to walk, laugh, hear, or see. There would probably be little about a child reared in isolation that we could call human. We are not assured of becoming human when we are born. The infant severed from the umbilical cord trails no clouds of glory. Deprived of social contact it would become neither animal nor human. Its movements would be strange, its expression bizarre, its sounds unrecognizable. Though perfectly shaped it would be a mythical monster. Most of the traits we call human are achieved after birth as the result of example, training, education—in other words, as the result of enculturation. Unlike the lower animals, humans are capable of acquiring culture.

The behavior of the lower animals is in large part instinctive. Rather than learned, it is programmed in the genes. A spider does not have to learn to spin a web or a bear to hibernate. Homing birds bred in the United States for six generations that have never seen the ocean will fly safely across the Atlantic to the home of their ancestors in England. The behavior of humans, however, is in large part learned from other humans after birth.

What Is Culture? We will define culture as the total pattern of learned human behavior. It includes among other things the way we work, listen, keep clean, play games, hiss, or applaud. It is also the products of human behavior whether fishhooks, hot dogs, nuclear reactors, or institutions such as the family and the church. It is in addition the products of thinking such as $E=MC^2$, *Hamlet,* a new rock song, or the gods of ancient Babylon. Encompassing the whole spectrum of human thought and imagination, culture is the people-made part of the envi-

People rarely eat only because of hunger. They must eat at the right place, in the right company, and at the right time. Americans take a coffee break; the Dutch take a herring break. Eating is not just putting food in one's mouth; it involves a preference for certain substances cooked or uncooked in certain ways. The Vedda people of Ceylon eat rotted wood garnished with honey. Hindus may not eat meat, Eskimos eat little else. Orthodox Jews may not eat pork, eel, camel, or rabbit. In the United States over a three-day holiday people will consume over 220 million hot dogs. In the western Pacific people shun hot dogs, which they think of as fat worms. Food is what a particular culture says it is. • A farmer and his family in Dahomey, West Africa, dine on grated cassava (manioc) and mice.

ronment. Culture is not the tree in the forest but the totem pole we make of it.

Nearly every human act, whether voluntary or involuntary, is influenced by the patterns of behavior common to our society. Even our digestive juices run on a time table that is set by our family, class, economic standing, tribe, or nation. How often we feel hungry in the course of the day, how many meals we eat, with whom we eat, in what posture we eat, and what we eat—all are conditioned by our culture. We may be starving and yet we cannot bring ourselves to place in our mouths that which our culture designates as disgusting. Scrambled eggs and bacon are a great breakfast dish for Americans. But to

Moslems bacon is revolting and to some East Africans eggs scrambled or otherwise are nauseating. A New Guinean cannibal will eat human flesh; yet he turns up his nose at frankfurters, which he regards as giant worms. Nowhere does eating alone satisfy hunger. Everywhere culture presides over the table.

Drives of sexuality as well as drives of hunger are governed by the customary way of doing things in our society. What we regard as erotically stimulating is tempered by body covering or the lack of it, or the shape of ears, nose, lips, feet, or genitals. Invading our sleeping life, culture influences not only our posture but also the content of our most secret dreams. Standing, walking, sitting, or gesturing all take cues from our culture. We may take our ease standing on two feet firmly planted on the ground about twelve inches apart. But some Nilotic African peoples relax standing on one foot, with the other placed on the knee of the anchor foot.

A number of reflex actions are influenced by culture. Western peoples shun pain; but in the South Pacific and elsewhere fire walkers, seemingly immune to pain, step barefoot over rocks heated to an incandescent glow. Blushing varies from society to society. Americans blush in the face; other peoples blush in the chest, arms, or other parts of the body.

Culture as Organization Actually none of us learns culture; rather we learn a particular culture, the behaviorial pattern of the society into which we happen to be born. Removed from the wilderness and introduced to the company of human beings, Victor learned not culture in general but the culture of urban France in the early nineteenth century. He learned to respond not to language in general but to the French language, just as he learned to respond to French food, manners, and customs. Culture has no existence apart from society.

As we learn our culture a number of benefits accrue to us. Whether in our family, employment, school, or on the street we meet a good many people: strangers, friends, business associates, relatives. We manage to get through the day with a minimum of friction because our culture tells us what kind of behavior we can expect of each of them. A culture is a chart of social anticipations. Knowing the rules, cues, and taboos we steer our way through a maze of social encounters just as a driver who knows his manual gets through heavy traffic without a smashup. Jostled in a crowd we say "Excuse me" and pass on. In our society we are expected to avoid violence even when provoked. Aware of the expectations of his tribe, even a ferocious Yanomamö exchanges blows with his open palm or fist before he picks up his axe. Culture helps maintain social order by giving people a reasonable idea of what to expect of each other.

We have said that culture is learned behavior. But more than that, it is usually a pattern of behavior with an internal organization of its own. Like a jigsaw piece that has fallen from the table, a custom seen by itself may seem peculiar. But reinserted into its proper place in the social structure, it makes sense. Observed by itself, a dramatic puberty rite may appear monstrous. But associated with the necessity in a hunting and fighting society of severing the strong bond between mother and son, it becomes meaningful.

That a Hopi husband who sees his personal belongings piled outside the door can without further ado take leave of his wife and go back to his mother's home must strike outside observers as strange. That is, until we discover how weak are the ties that hold husband and wife together in Hopi society. In our culture a spouse's first allegiance is to his or her family. Among the Hopi a person traces his descent through the female line. A husband's first allegiance therefore is to his mother's family; a wife's first allegiance is to her mother's family. A husband is a member of his mother's kin group, to which he is tied by economic, social, and religious obligations. The fields in which he works, the tools he uses, the house in which he lives are not his, but his wife's. All his married life he is a sojourner in another's home.

Only when we become aware of the strength of the female lineage principle among the Hopi can we begin to understand how fragile is the bond between husband and wife and how easily it can be dissolved. The Hopi culture like any other is no hodgepodge of human behavior but a fairly consistent and sensible arrangement of interrelated customs, practices, beliefs, and institutions. A culture is more than the sum of its parts.

Though there is constant pressure toward consistency in any society, we know that all customs do not necessarily fit, nor are they all equally meaningful. In some cases they may be positively lethal. The enforced chastity of the religious community of the Shakers eventually reduced the order to near zero population. The continuing pollution of the air, water, and food by industrial states endangers health and life. A living culture is not a perfect machine. Yet though the gears may sometimes grind and growl, they will usually mesh.

The Whole Earth Catalog of Culture Culture both frees and binds. Through technology and tool use, culture liberates people from backbreaking toil and releases their energies for art, music, and other creative activities. On the other hand, culture through law, custom, and conscience restricts the total freedom of the individual and keeps variations in behavior within acceptable bounds. In no society can anyone do as he pleases. Jonathan Miller may rig himself in grotesque garb for his fraternity initiation, but he may not publicly divest himself of all his clothing.

Over a period of more than one hundred thousand years the present human species on the planet, *Homo sapiens,* has accumulated a vast catalog of possible behavior from which each society has—in a sense—made its own selection in order to meet the demands of its physical and social environment. The American life style, like the Arunta life style, is only one particular manifestation of human behavior. The American anthropologist Alfred Kroeber once estimated that no society provides an outlet for more than 3 or 4 percent of the potential behavior of its members. Which is just as well, for if people behaved in all the ways of which the species is capable, the results would be bedlam. The limitation on behavior is the first law of living in society.

Drastically reducing possible alternatives, each society encourages the expression of some human traits and ignores or penalizes the acting out of others. In the United States little encouragement is usually given to people who fall into trancelike states and see or hear things that are not there. Such people are often labeled mentally ill and placed under the care of a person in a white coat.* In Haiti, however, spirit possession is considered normal, not psychopathic. In a large number of tribal communities a shaman is required to demonstrate his ability to fall into a trance and communicate with the spirits.

Ethnocentrism In all societies people may become so convinced of the correctness of their behavioral choices that they become the vassals of their culture, unable to perceive anything admirable beyond their gates. Westerners often think that worshippers of more gods than one are heathen, that polygamous families are promiscuous, or that tribal peoples are ignorant. Similarly, non-Western people are frequently put off by the customs of Europeans and Americans. To the Japanese the American arrangement of having bath facilities and toilet in the same room is offensive. To some tribal peoples the Western habit of kissing on the mouth is repulsive. "Whites eat each other's saliva," they say. On the island of Samoa a European who used his napkin in full view of the other guests would be considered extremely rude. A well-mannered guest placed his hands behind his back before wiping them.

Because our culture is learned so early in life—long before we know of other ways of living—we tend to take it for granted and to think of it as the only proper way of thinking, feeling,

* In charismatic worship, however, the exorcising of demons from a spellbound victim is encouraged in healing services.

and behaving. We view the life styles of other peoples as though we were looking into a parabolic mirror at the circus. What we do seems normal and natural, but what others do often seems unnatural, bizarre, and contrary to common sense.

In every society people refer to themselves in complimentary terms and to outsiders in derogatory language. Eskimos call themselves *Innuit,* which means "we alone are human." The name *Hopi* signifies "good in every respect." The Cheyenne referred to themselves as "the people," designating other tribes as non-persons. In America terms such as *Polack, wop, kike, spic, nigger, squarehead,* signify the alleged inferiority of various minorities.

Anthropologists like to steer clear of the term *primitive* to describe people in tribal communities because it implies that they are simple-minded, irresponsible, and ignorant, supposedly survivors of the Old Stone Age for whom time has stood still, in contrast to Western people who have marched ahead and forged the great contemporary "civilizations." But what distinguishes industrial societies from tribal societies is technology and social complexity not intelligence, maturity, wisdom, or morals. Though Westerners have amassed knowledge on an unprecedented scale and made astounding discoveries in science, it is questionable that they excel a number of small-scale societies in music, declamation, poetry, art, and other expressive aspects of life. The "primitive" Arunta whose three basic tools are a lance, a spear thrower, and a digging stick possess myths and traditions of amazing richness and sensitivity. Despite the rudimentary level of their material life, they have, according to Lévi-Strauss, "a taste for erudition and speculation few societies can equal."

We as individuals and as a nation often think we are the strongest, the bravest, the wisest and the best. In that attitude we unconsciously cover up and fail to acknowledge our mistakes.

—Jimmy Carter, President of the United States, 1977

Ethnocentrism is the almost universal belief that one's own

culture provides an absolute standard against which all others are to be judged. It follows that one's own society is superior to all others so that there is only one right way of family organization, sanitation, government, sexual behavior, and eating. Carried to its extreme limits ethnocentrism may lead to gross discrimination and savagery toward an ethnic minority which may be treated as though it fell outside the range of humanity. Recently in Colombia, South America, a gang of cattlemen pleaded not guilty to the charge of massacring a band of Indians on the ground that killing Indians was not a crime.

Western people often find it difficult to understand why tribal and peasant peoples should cling so tenaciously to their way of life when the American or European way is so obviously "superior." Why do these "primitive" people so often fail to appreciate the introduction of Western hospitals, education, or food? In western Africa missionaries who built a Western-type hospital were amazed to discover that patients were sleeping under their beds. The missionaries could not comprehend that the patients were accustomed to sleeping on the floor. In Iran a Western public health team built open showers somewhat like those found in an American locker room only to discover that no one would use them. What the experts had not taken into account was that Iranian males are ashamed about appearing naked in each other's presence. Misguided by preconceptions of how they think people ought to act, technical experts who bring aid to underdeveloped countries sometimes fail to appreciate the culture of those whom they want to help.

If the Great Spirit had desired me to be a white man he would have made me so in the first place. He put into your heart certain wishes and plans; in my heart he put other and different desires. Each man is good in his sight. It is not necessary for eagles to be crows.

—Sitting Bull, Sioux Indian chief

Culture Change One characteristic of culture is that it never stands still. In a small-scale isolated society change may be so slow that it is almost imperceptible. In a contemporary industrial state, change is constantly accelerating. Impermanence has become one of the expectations of Western culture. For many Westerners the worst that can happen is that nothing has happened. Americans can sympathize with the man who, Thoreau said, lay down for a ten-minute nap and on awakening asked, "What's new?"

Culture change is the process by which people absorb new ideas, values, institutions, and the use of new objects, modifying their behavior accordingly. A new cultural element arouses a storm of resistance and controversy today. By the end of the year the storm has died down and in a few years what was once new may be fully acceptable. The long hair that shocked fathers and schoolmasters in the sixties became an adult fashion in the seventies.

Institutions such as the family are rapidly changing. As a result of the climbing divorce rate in America, and the growing tendency of young people to marry later and put off having children, half of all households in the United States at the present time consist of single persons or married persons without children. The concept of the family in which "the husband is the only breadwinner, the wife is the homemaker, and there are children" is today an accurate description of only seven out of every one hundred households in the country.*

As an institution changes so does its definition. Under the revised regulations of the United States Department of Housing and Urban Development a family now consists of "two or more persons sharing residency whose income and resources are available to meet the family's needs and who are related by blood, marriage or operation of law or have evidenced a stable family relationship." All of which means that for the purpose of securing public housing the government will regard heterosexual and/or homosexual unmarried people with or without chil-

* U.S. Department of Labor, April 8, 1977.

As the pace of Westernization quickens, pre-industrial cultures come face to face with new ways of life. • Top, in Swaziland in southern Africa, a census taker interviews a tribal chieftain. Bottom, until recently one of the most primitive regions on earth, New Guinea is now acquiring some of the problems of industrial cultures. A policeman directs traffic at Port Moresby, Papua, on the eastern side of New Guinea.

dren as a family. It may not be long before the students who were evicted from a street zoned for one-family living will be able to move back.

Invention and Diffusion Invention and discovery help to bring about culture change. Invention may refer to a material object like the wheel or the computer. It may also refer to a new idea like the calendar, a new form of art, or an innovation in political or social organization. The introduction of a new object or idea may have a profound influence on many aspects of a culture. The coming of the automobile not only revolutionized transportation in America but created new industries, spread the population into the countryside, and altered many forms of recreation.

I've been divorced five years. When I was married I ate out maybe twice a week. Now I eat out five nights a week. I like to be with people.

—A Kansas City air line executive, 1977

Changes in family structure are changing America's way of eating. The growth of the singles culture has encouraged eating out. In addition, in married households half of all wives now work, thereby making family income available for a meal away from home. New tendencies in the American family have helped create a new industry, the fast-food restaurant.

Every culture changes with invention and discovery, but no culture is responsible for all the inventions and discoveries it uses. All cultures borrow from one nother. It is hard to hide a cultural secret.

We Americans generally like to feel that we are the inventors and others are the borrowers. But as a new nation we have probably borrowed far more than we have created. In his essay "One Hundred Percent American" American anthropologist Ralph Linton provides numerous examples of borrowing cultural elements from other societies:

". . . if it looks like rain [the average American] puts on outer shoes of rubber discovered by the ancient Mexicans and takes an umbrella invented in India. At the station he buys a newpaper, paying for it in coins invented in ancient Lydia. Once on board his train he settles back to inhale the fumes of a cigar invented in Brazil. Meanwhile he reads the news in characters invented by the ancient Semites by a process invented in Germany upon a material invented in China. As he scans the latest editorial . . . he will not fail to thank a Hebrew God in an Indo-European tongue that he is a one hundred percent (decimal point invented by the Greeks) American (from Americus Vespucci, Italian geographer.)"

Diffusion is a process by which cultural elements spread from one society to another—whether fashion, foods, songs, or plumbing. The Plains Indians, for example, did not invent the idea of riding the horse but adopted the idea plus the saddle, reins, and bit from the Spanish invaders.

The mere knowledge of the existence of a cultural element in another society may stimulate the invention of a similar practice or object in one's own. In the 1820s a remarkably gifted illiterate Cherokee Indian named Sequoya noticed that the whites were able to read. Borrowing the idea of a writing system from them, he invented his own alphabet to represent the sounds of the Cherokee language. Adopted by the Cherokee, Sequoya's writing system is in use to this day.

Once started, a cultural item can find its way around the world. Grimm's fairy tale known as "The Musicians of Bremen" in which a number of animals outwit a pack of robbers evidently appeared in India at least one thousand years ago. Crossing many language barriers it was diffused by word of mouth around the world. From India it traveled into southern Russia, up through Central Europe, and into Germany, where it arrived in the Middle Ages. After the colonization of America white trappers spread it among the Indians, the tribes of the Plains giving it a new twist in a version called "Big Turtle's War Party."

Diffusion of culture elements from industrial society has altered the life of tribal people all over the world. • An Eskimo couple in their igloo in the Canadian Yukon are surrounded by the artifacts of Western civilization.

Acculturation Not only invention and diffusion but acculturation can bring about change in a society. Acculturation, or the wholesale absorption of culture elements, occurs when the culture of a weaker society is drastically changed by contact with a more powerful society. For example, the military and economic expansion of Western nations since the time of Columbus has led to the imposition of their dress, languages, music, recreation and many other culture elements on pre-industrial peoples throughout the globe. Not necessarily coercive, acculturation may be welcomed by weaker societies who hope to share some of the benefits of Western technologies and life styles.

In its extreme form acculturation can become detribalization or the outright destruction of a culture. In Mexico the Spanish conquerors forced the Indians to accept their religion and way of life and at the same time tried to wipe out the native culture by razing the great pyramids and temples and burning ancient historical records. In the western United States after the extermination of the buffalo herds on which their native economy depended, the Indians had to give up much of their culture and accept that of the whites in order to survive.

> Then everything was good.
> There was no sin; there was no sickness.
> There were no aching bones.
> The course of humanity was orderly.
> The white men brought shameful things with them:
> The beginning of our misery.
>
> —*A Mayan Indian lamenting the destruction of his ancient culture*

In recent years the Eskimo have absorbed white cultural items that range from ice cream and mail-order clothing to schooling and snowmobiles. But the coming of the whites has also resulted in the detribalization of most of the Eskimos. To make room for roads, oil rigs, and pipelines the whites have killed off many of the fish, muskrats, caribou, and other animals on which the Eskimos relied for food and clothing. Forced to leave the wilderness, formerly self-reliant hunters and gatherers now live in urban and rural slums where only the welfare check keeps many from starvation.

Some tribal peoples, although they still live in their native territories, experience a sense of deep foreboding as "civilization" each year presses closer. A visitor recently asked the chieftain of a Xingu Indian village what he wanted his son to be. The chieftain thought for a while and then replied: "I would like him to be a famous shaman like his uncle. I would like him to be a skilled hunter like his older brother. I would like him to be a leader of his people like me. Yes, I would like him to be all of these things. But he will be none of them. The road is coming and that will be the end of us all." The chief was referring to a spur of the Trans-Amazonian highway being built a few miles away, leveling the rain forest, driving off the game, and bringing in its wake thousands of white settlers, prospectors, and cattlemen. The ancient way of life of the Xinguanos is threatened.

In South America, Africa, and Australia, as well as in the Arctic, the result of acculturation has been a loss of purpose in life for many tribal peoples. Asked why he drank, a seventeen-year-old Cree Indian in northern Quebec replied, "What else is there to do?" Removed from their land, rituals, and traditions, many Indians live in extreme poverty on the edge of the white man's cities. Their living conditions reflect not their original culture but some of the most degrading aspects of Western civilization.

In the beginning God gave to every people a cup, a cup of clay, and from the cup they drank their life. They all dipped into the water but their cups were different. Our cup is broken now. It is passed away.

—*A California Indian's remark to Ruth Benedict, American anthropologist*

Overcome by despair many commit suicide. Mothers may induce miscarriage and neglect their living children. Sometimes mild diseases become fatal illnesses. The family, the very essence of tribal community, is often broken up. With the loss of their culture people lose the will to live: their cup of life is broken.

In the process of acculturation tribal people may acquire alcoholism, unemployment, and reliance on welfare from the dominant culture. They may also acquire other traits of the dominant culture such as trade unionism, political activism, and legal action for the redress of grievances. While some tribal peoples have expressed their protest in revitalization movements, others have begun to use the political, social, and economic skills of the whites to win back a part of what they have lost.

There is a voice crying in the wilderness but it is no longer a voice crying for pity. It is a cry against the average age span of forty-four years, against the suicide rate of teen-agers on reservations that is three times that of teenagers in general, against the alcoholism rate, against the arrest rate. It is the war cry of a people who seek their humanity.

—*James Lee West, a Cheyenne Indian, 1975*

In search of a better life, tribal people in the Arctic, Australia, and Africa migrate to urban centers where they are forced to live in slums without adequate housing, food, sanitation, or employment. • A pondokis, *or squatter settlement, in the southern suburbs of Cape Town, Republic of South Africa.*

In different parts of the world there are tribal people who instead of waiting patiently for the Millennium are filing briefs in the courts, organizing trade unions, and voting in elections. In the United States a number of Indian groups have succeeded in recovering some of their land, saving their water rights, and enforcing old treaties. To get the conqueror off their backs they are making the conqueror's culture work for them.

In the contemporary industrial society so rapid is the speed of cultural change that we can see it occurring before our eyes. Let us now look at some of the startling changes in sexual behavior and attitudes that have taken place in the last decade or two.

the sexual revolution

13

"She's a Perfectly Normal Human Being"

THE sex act is the most private of all human activities; yet all societies make it the public's business. Where, when, under what circumstances, and with whom one shall have sex are all subject to law, regulation, and custom. Peoples differ vastly about the degree of sexual leeway they allow, the range extending from the encouragement of youthful experimentation and wife exchange to the extension of the incest taboo to the most distant cousins.

> I find that the three major problems on campus are sex for the students, athletics for the alumni, and parking for the faculty.
>
> —*Clark Kerr, President of the University of California*

Restrictive America Every society is convinced that its particular way of managing sexuality is proper and natural. Until the 1960s America was, at least in theory, one of the most restrictive societies on earth. Virginity was cherished for females, and chastity expected of them until they married. Sexual expression belonged only within the institution of marriage. Sex

Formerly a highly restrictive society, the United States appears on the way to becoming one of the more permissive. Both the young and the old are assailed by the blatant display of sexuality not only in the movies, on the stage, and in books and periodicals but also in advertising.

was a topic parents did not discuss comfortably with their children. During the course of his study of "Plainview," a small town in Missouri, the sociologist Carl Withers was told, "People around here do not like to talk about that," meaning that anything referring to human sexuality was a source of embarrassment. Though the children of "Plainview" lived in a farm community where they frequently witnessed the copulation of pigs, cows, and sheep, they were put off by their parents whenever they asked questions. Later they were to learn from their peers the secrets their parents had hidden from them.

Children in urban communities often received their first sex briefings in the local candy store where according to Art Buchwald:

". . . the information was dispensed by thirteen-year-olds who seemed to know everything there was to know. . . . For example I was told that if a girl necked with you in the rumble seat of a car she would automatically have a baby. This kept me out of the rumble seat of an automobile until I was twenty-three years old."

The New Permissiveness But as the song says, "The times they are a-changin'." The introduction of sex education in the schools accompanied by a new permissiveness for both young and old marks a significant alteration in the American life style. The old restrictions fall away one by one: Respectable hotels accept guests who insist on registering as unmarried couples. Municipalities that formerly jailed the proprietors of massage parlors, striptease shows, topless bars, and "blue" movie theatres may now allow them to do business in zoned pornography areas. Ocean and lake resorts may set aside nudist beaches for those who want all-over tans. Explicit sex scenes appear in serious films as well as in current plays. In Nevada the madam of a legal house of prostitution runs for office in the state legislature under the slogan "I cannot be bought." (She was not elected.) What is decent or indecent, proper or shameful, moral or immoral, has undergone sweeping revision in the last two decades.

Since the sixties public opinion pollsters have scurried around the country to record changes in sexual attitudes and behavior. A 1975 poll indicated that almost half of all unmarried women had sexual relations before they were twenty. Among married high school graduates half the females and 85 percent of the males reported that they had engaged in sexual relations prior to marriage. Of those forty years or older, one out of every four women and one out of every two men polled had had extramarital affairs. In another survey in the same year more than 80 percent of all young middle-class women polled had had premarital sex—most of them before the age of eighteen. After marriage almost a third reported having sex with partners other than their husbands. One startling finding of the pollsters was that one-third of all brides aged eighteen or younger were pregnant at the time of marriage. A girl in a southern university said, "I don't know a girl who will not sleep with a boy unless they are married, but I know only a handful of girls who will sleep with boys they don't care for."

Age seems to be no barrier to people living together without being married. The partners are as likely to be the elderly who are combining their Social Security income as young people. The Census Bureau has estimated an eightfold increase within a ten-year period in the category it calls "Partners of the Opposite Sex Sharing Living Quarters."

Together with the acceptance of greater permissiveness in heterosexual behavior has come a more tolerant attitude toward homosexuality. Gay clubs appear on college campuses. In California, where sodomy was formerly punishable by life imprisonment, private sexual acts by consenting individuals are no longer criminal. A few way-out churches offer homosexual couples the sanctity of a religious ceremony.

> Boulder, Colorado: A few weeks ago two persons from Colorado Springs obtained without fanfare a marriage license from the County Clerk's office here. Then they were married. The wedding would have passed unnoticed except that the partners were homosexual men. . . . To demonstate his disgust one local cowboy marched to the County Clerk's office last week with a request to marry his favorite horse. The request was denied on the ground that the horse, an eight-year-old mare, was underage.
>
> —New York Times, *1975*

American parents in the past discouraged the sexual activities of their teen-age children, though they were far more concerned about the chastity of their daughters than of their sons. While boys were sowing their wild oats girls were expected to go horseback riding. Today increasing numbers of parents casually accept the news that their daughter has shacked up with a young man. Asked how she would feel if her daughter told her she was having an affair, a mother replied, "I wouldn't be surprised; she's a perfectly normal human being." The remark would not be especially significant except that it was made by the wife of a President of the United States. Like the Trobriand

Young people in the United States are expressing their sexuality at a younger age than ever before. Illegitimacy among white girls in their mid-teens rose by nearly 50 percent in the decade 1965–1975, probably because their increased sexual activity was not accompanied by widespread use of contraception.

Islanders or the Kadar of Nigeria, many Americans no longer set great store in premarital chastity.

Q. How do unmarried couples usually refer to one another?
A. Terms range from hyperlegal (my coinhabitant) to the hypercute (my roommate) and with the overwhelming being the old standby—"my friend."
Q. What about introductions? . . .
A. To the tradition-minded relative, "This is Jane, a friend of John's." To the broadminded relative: "This is Jane, who is sharing an apartment with John."

—*New York Times, 1977*

Cultural elements are closely interrelated. Innovations in sexual behavior have been accompanied by changes in marriage patterns and family structure. Once traditionally "for life," marriage in America has become a transient experience for a considerable portion of the population. In 1976 there was almost one divorce for every two marriages, the number of marriages ending in divorce exceeding the million mark for the first time in the nation's history. Although the polygamist must continue to remain underground, most Americans can marry as many times as they wish, provided that they are married to only one spouse at a time.

In a society devoted to the family ideal of every adult married to a loving mate, there were in 1975 43 million marriageable though unmarried citizens. Many have given up trying to find Mr. Right or Miss Wonderful; others do not seem to care. For a growing subculture of single men and women in their late twenties, thirties, and forties living alone without a permanent mate, marriage no longer appears to be a prerequisite to emotional and social maturity.

> "We were talking about a girl's name the other night," said Mrs. Terranova. "First Bernie said, 'It doesn't have to sound good with our name because it will change anyhow when she gets married.' I said, 'Who knows, in twenty years girls will not change their names. Our daughter may not even get married. The world's changing; we'll raise her to be independent.' "
>
> —New York Times, *1976*

Tradition and Sexuality What has brought about such profound changes in the sexual attitudes and behavior of many Americans? Undoubtedly the antibiotic treatment of sexually transmitted diseases and the availability of abortion, the "pill," sterilization, and other contraceptive techniques have encouraged freer sexual expression. That humans are now able to dissociate the sexual act from reproduction with almost complete certainty has been one of the most startling scientific discoveries of the twentieth century—and a neat example of how invention can spark social change.

At the same time young people are becoming the most informed generation about sex America has ever known. Subjects once unmentionable both at home and at school such as contraception, sexual deviancy, abortion, and veneral disease are discussed in college and secondary school classrooms. New texts, courses of study, and films on sex education become available almost every day. Were he going to school today, Art Buchwald would have few anxieties about getting into the rumble seat of a car with a girl.

The sexual revolution may also be seen as a reaction to a restrictive morality that dominated America for three hundred years. Among the traditions that the country inherited from past experience were such ideals as those of hard work, frugality, and self-denial. These were basic values that helped the early settlers conquer the native population, set up their own form of European civilization in the wilderness, and eventually free themselves of the mother country.

To the Puritans sexuality for purposes other than procreation within the institution of Holy Matrimony was a sin that interfered not only with their goal of worldly success but their reception into Heaven among God's Elect. Forms of pleasure that we would consider quite innocent such as May Pole dances, Christmas festivities, sports, and games were highly suspect. Idle talk and ostentatious display were considered immoral. In their churches the Puritans rejected sculpture, paintings, and other sensuous aspects of worship because worldly things might distract from the veneration of God. Right conduct included the wise use of time, thrift, and industry as well as sabbath observance. The daily round of living was replete with religious significance.

The Puritan ethic together with the attitudes of both the Catholic and Protestant churches played a large role in shaping the sexual behavior of Americans. But as a culture changes, many of its values are bound to be altered. In the technological transformation from nineteenth-century agrarianism to twentieth-century industrialism, America has become one of the most affluent societies on earth. Early ideals that promoted thrift, frugality, and abstinence have been forced into the background by an economy that hails consumerism, big spending, and the production of products once considered mere show. The prosperity of the nation depends less on saving than on spending. The voices of the past are drowned in the din of the commercials which urge the viewer to make a big splash, own not one but two cars, run up bills, apply for a loan at his friendly neighborhood bank, and then apply for a second loan to pay the first.*

The pursuit of pleasure is a deep concern in the contemporary world. Even before they enter school, children absorb the

* As America uses up scarce resources and imperils the natural environment, the Puritan value of "waste not, want not" begins to look good again.

idea that accomplishment should be laced with amusement. "Sesame Street" teaches the numbers one to ten to the accompaniment of pratfalls, jokes, singing, and cookie monsters. In high school and college serious study is rendered palatable with generous helpings of fraternity parties, football spectaculars, rock concerts, bridge tournaments, and faculty jesters. As every salesman with an expense account knows, mixing business and pleasure promotes the sale of products and services and keeps the economy healthy.

The sexual revolution may be viewed as one aspect of a fundamental shift in American values toward hedonism, the doctrine that pleasure represents the highest good. For some people it has become the principal reason for living. A person has not really lived until he has snorkeled, eaten at a four-star restaurant, visited Opryland, or slept with a variety of partners.

People seek the maximization of sexual expression as they do other forms of pleasure. Instead of feeling guilty about enjoying sex, they feel guilty if they do not enjoy it enough. Those "unfortunates" who cannot make the grade seek help from a whole new profession of sexual therapists. Once highly suspect, sexual pleasure has become, for many, a moral obligation.

In a highly industrialized society individual spontaneity and impulse must frequently give way to the pace of the machine and the demands of the factory and office. Freedom is experienced not at work, but in the realm of personal relationships where sexual adventures seem to offer relief from the tedium of everyday routine. Recently, as the boundaries of civil liberties have expanded in America, so have the boundaries of private liberties. Unlike the totalitarian state, a democratic society can absorb a wide range of behavior, both public and personal. Sexual relationships could not remain forever tied to a restrictive tradition.

Where Is the Sexual Revolution Going? In the last twenty years probably no cultural element in the United States has changed as radically as sexual behavior. Innovations which once dismayed the elders have become part of the current life style. Cultural change often begins with shock and ends with convention.

The anthropologist who works in a small-scale society can generally rely on what he observes about him and on what reliable informants tell him. In a vast industrial culture the social scientist must base his conclusions to a large extent on information garnered from surveys such as public opinion polls. These polls seem to be saying that the sexual revolution is more than a swing from restriction to permissiveness; it is also a reordering of the relations between men and women. Not only men but women now feel freer about expressing their sexuality. Sexual initiative, for example, is no longer an exclusively male prerogative.

The polls also indicate that young people are shedding much of the sense of sin and guilt that haunted previous generations. Some young people rather than rushing into marriages for which they may not be ready are maintaining intimate friendships and reserving marriage until the time they feel prepared to raise a family. Some people have gone though a period of premarital affairs and then retired to a kind of secondary virginity as though recognizing that they were incapable of handling total freedom.

Confronted with startling changes in erotic attitudes and behavior some Americans at first visualized the sexual revolution as an orgiastic leap into gross promiscuity. Actually, there is no danger that America will ever become a schoolboy's sexual fantasy. The chances are rather that Americans, as the 1972 White House Conference on Youth said, will increasingly come to look upon sexuality as a "sensitive, concerned, and responsible expression of human feeling."

Not every cultural innovation must find a permanent place in a society. We now consider the birth and subsequent disintegration of a counterculture in our own land.

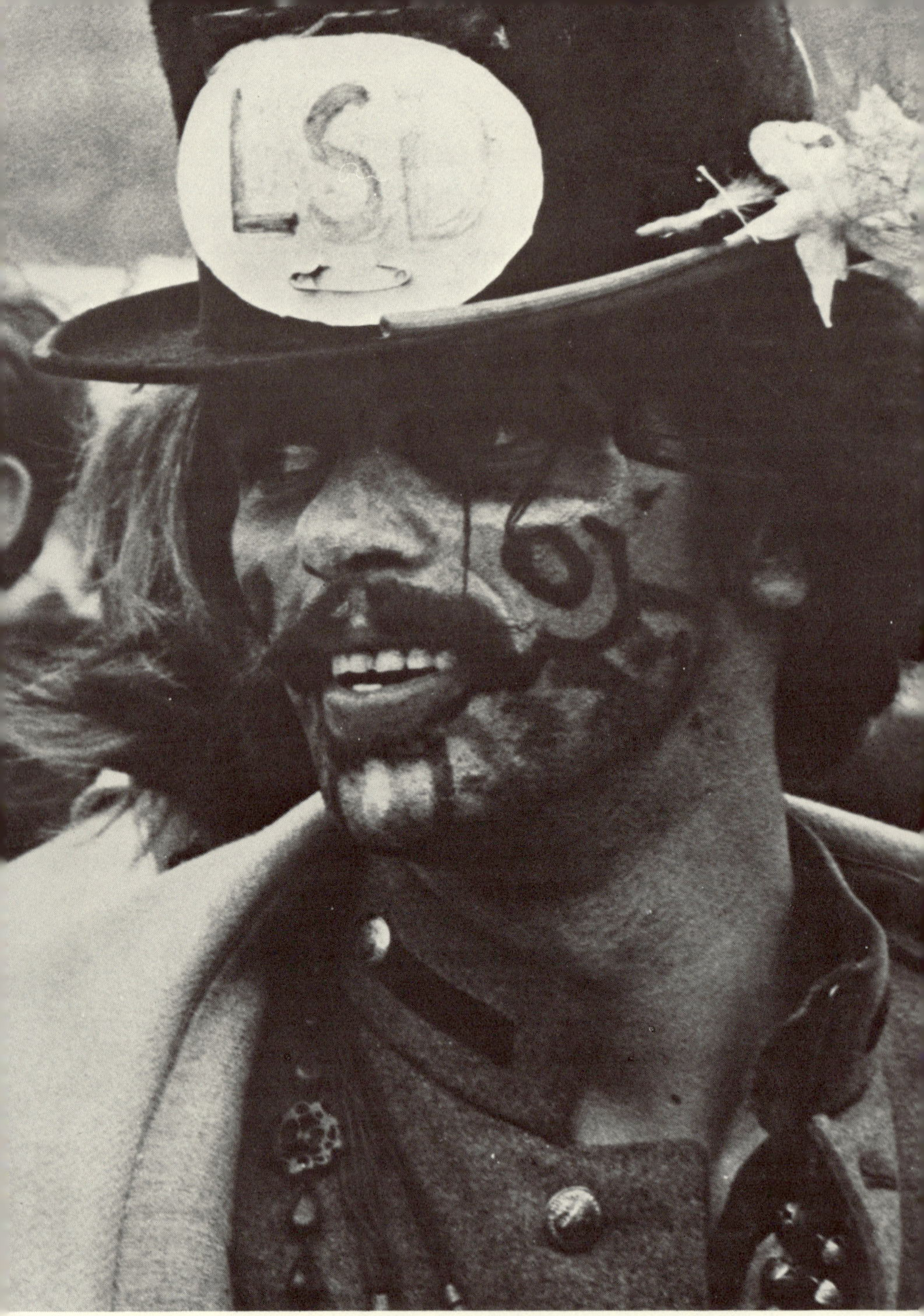
LSD

the youth movement

14

"Often Wondered What I Was, Then Who I Was, and Most Often, Why ME in a Human Shell"

ONCE upon a time in the far long ago of the midtwentieth century there was no Haight-Ashbury or East Village; there was no counterculture; there was no mass youth movement. Then in the tumultuous days of the 1960s the youth of America suddenly became visible. Stealing the headlines from politics, finance, and international affairs, they seized university buildings; picketed the Pentagon; swarmed at rock festivals; and paraded the streets in the garb of frontiersmen, Civil War soldiers, Indians, and holy men.

Some young people abandoning home and school embarked on a continuous holiday, skiing in Colorado, surfing in Hawaii, sunbathing on the beaches of Goa in India, oblivious to everything but pleasure. Some joined the Peace Corps or campaigned for civil rights in the South, coming to terms with themselves by helping others. Some fled to Canada to avoid fighting a war in which they did not believe. Some joined the sex and drug scene in New York or in San Francisco, living in communal groups and by example preventing each other from deserting.

Each year new groups caught the public eye. Beats, hippies, flower children, Yippies, motorcycle gangsters, or rock and rollers, they saw themselves not as second-year students, gasoline attendants, or taxi drivers, but as mystics, prophets, troubadors of the open road, or tigers in souped-up cars. The youth movement was never one crusade but dozens of scattered life ways: religious, revolutionary, utopian, or drug fixated. What the young people had in common was their antagonism to the larger American culture and a devotion to rock music, which brought them together in mammoth festivals that bore little resemblance to Boy Scout jamborees. Though born in America, the movement quickly spread to Holland, Germany, Japan, and other industrial countries.

Culture and Subculture Collectively the assorted youth of the sixties whose behavior and appearance set them apart from the majority of Americans formed a subculture within the larger society. In a small-scale isolated society everyone, adults and young people, follows the same life style. Everyone in a Yanomamö community worships the same gods, recognizes the same manners, eats the same diet, and shares the same amusements. Culture and life style are one.

In a complex industrial society such as America, there are many life styles: suburban, ghetto, jet set, trailer camp, gypsy, Puerto Rican. America is multicultural, a vast supermarket of subcultures within the larger culture. One subculture easily distinguished from the life style of the rest of us is the Old Order Amish of Indiana, Ohio, and Pennsylvania who try to live as they did when they migrated from Europe in 1827. The Amish refuse to use cars, telephones, or electricity, and dress in broad-brimmed hats and plain buttonless clothes. They will not fight in any war or send their children to high school.

We dress plainly not to please ourselves but to remind us to keep God's commandments and to remind us who and what we are.

—*An Amish minister, 1976*

The industrially advanced societies found in North America display an array of subcultures. • Top, the Mennonites attempt to live like their ancestors and adhere to values and dress that easily set them apart from the general culture. Mennonites from Ontario, Canada. Bottom, in the slums of great cities ethnic groups set up their own subcultures. El Barrio, a Puerto Rican ghetto of Manhattan, New York City.

What brought about the youth subculture of the 1960s? There had been other youth movements in America in the past but these had been localized and of short duration. The sixties movement involved young people not only throughout the United States but in advanced industrial countries over the world. Comprising a population of 5½ million, the students who entered college in the sixties had been born during the baby boom following World War II. Campuses throughout the country were crowded with young people including graduate students and dropouts who hung around without attending classes. It was the time of the Vietnam war and many students subject to the draft elected to stay in college rather than be caught up in an unpopular war.

As the need for prolonged technical training increased with the growing industrialization of the nation, students spent more time in school and less time with their families. In many cases they became more closely identified with school life than with home life. It is likely that the enforced separation from the adult community together with an enforced association with the student community created a sense of group awareness among young people. Segregated from the rest of society and interacting primarily with each other, young people in the sixties began to see themselves as part of a youth culture with common goals and common interests. Adopting a mode of dress, speech, and behavior that set them off from other Americans, they established a distinct life style of their own.

The requirements for admission were minimal; the rules, few. An initiate did not have to be attractive, tidy, slim, or at the top of his class. Who his parents were, whether he had a car, whether he knew how to order in a restaurant, did not matter. All he had to be was to be himself. All he had to do was to do his own thing. As popular songs of the sixties promised: "All you need is love/Say the word *love* and you'll be free/Let it be/Everything will be all right." As the youth movement flung wide its doors to all comers, sorority and fraternity membership shrank disastrously.

An enormous body of youth set apart from the rest of the society and aware of its identity may yet have remained relatively quiescent but for two factors: the struggle in the sixties for civil liberties for blacks and the Vietnam war. For thousands of students the civil rights campaigns were the beginning of political and social consciousness. Civil rights became a rallying cry that tested the sense of fairness and idealism of many young people.

The battle for racial justice was a source of moral anguish. Vietnam, on the other hand, was a real threat. Some students burned their draft cards; some refused to serve and went to jail; some fled to Canada. Other students engaged in vigils and mass rallies, picketed, boycotted classes, and seized campus buildings. Vietnam radicalized a good many young people.

One student protest in Berkeley or at Cornell set tremors going in Berlin, Tokyo, Paris, and Rome. Students watched each other admiringly and at times copied each other's actions. An age of instantaneous communication exposed them to world events with a speed and immediacy unlike anything in the past. The youth movement was international in scope.

The Alienated and the Drugged The youth culture was large enough in scope to encompass those who dropped out of school or never continued their education. Its minimal requirements held a special attraction for young people who were overwhelmed by a feeling of alienation, that is, a sense of disconnectedness or isolation with which they could not cope. Estranged from community and family these youths experienced an emotional gap between themselves and those who might have been expected to love and help them.

> No one to talk to, they don't want to listen, never had anything important to say anyhow. Growing up, growing up alone, grew up lonely. Only friends I ever had were the wind and the sea. Haven't seen my father in nearly . . .
>
> —*An American youth in the 1960s*

Their speech was symptomatic of their plight, tentative,

loose jointed, and hesitant, full of *like this* and *like that, man,* suggesting that they feared being pinned down to a positive statement. Bewildered, unable to accept responsibility, they drifted away from home, taking "in-and-out" jobs as they wandered over the states. Sometimes they gravitated toward Berkeley, Cambridge, Ann Arbor, and other university towns where they could be on campus yet remain free of academic discipline. Natural recruits for the new culture, they clung together for companionship and created their own singular community.

Some of the alienated joined motorcycle gangs and other delinquent groups; others sought self-imposed seclusion. Rather than rebelling against the larger society, they tried to block it out. A few lived in mobile homes, hermetically sealing themselves off from most human contact. Traveling in a windowless van with his hi-fi turned up, a passenger heard and saw nothing of the outside world. "I don't want people looking in and I don't want to look out when I am riding in back," a youth said. "Everything you see looks the same. It's nicer just lying in back with a beer and the sounds."

Other young people drifted off toward a Nirvana within themselves, sloughing off an indifferent world with the aid of drugs. They were after "kicks," activities that intensified the present moment by differentiating it from humdrum experience. Provoking their elders by experimenting with the tabooed, they manufactured excitement with dirty syringes and overdoses. Doing their own thing, they often did themselves in. Throughout America suicide became the second most frequent cause of death among young people.

> I didn't have any way of finding out whether drugs were good or bad for me so I decided to try. I started shooting methedrine. One trip I took lasted nearly a fortnight. I didn't want to eat or sleep. When I crashed I was so weak I couldn't make it from the bed to the ice box. If a friend had not found me I think I would have died. I would have died like that, a few feet away from a can of beans.
>
> —*A seventeen-year-old on Haight Street, San Francisco, 1969*

Youth is a time of movement, and in the 1960s young people traveled as they never had before. Living on handouts from tourists or money orders from home, they would stop off for a while in such places as a Greek island, a Mexican village, Calcutta, Katmandu, Hawaii, Berlin, Seville, or Paris and then wander on. • Young travelers in Paris in 1969.

The Pleasure Seekers Many young people during the sixties took refuge in a hedonism that rudely contradicted the work ethic of their parents. Conventional Americans suppressed immediate gratification for the sake of future rewards. These young people saw no sense in putting off until tomorrow the fun they could have today: "If it feels good, do it; all that matters is here and now."

Instead of preparing for a career in some far-off time, they took ragtag jobs with hours they could control such as taxi driving, waiting on table, moving furniture, or street peddling (which in the sixties seemed to have become the monopoly of the young). They would work for a few days until they had enough to get by and then "make the scene" by socializing, having sex, plucking at a guitar, getting stoned at a rock festival, or reading Hesse, Vonnegut, Heinlein, or Tolkien. Unlike the vociferous hippies or the political activists, many of the pleasure seekers remained private persons known only to their parents, companions, and therapist. Keeping to themselves, they shunned outward rebellion and avoided the television camera.

The Counterculture In Western societies youth is the time when young people draw very close to each other. As they shrug off the bonds of family they willingly submit to the influence of gangs, clubs, and other peer associations. Nourished by the sense of fidelity and solidarity characteristic of the adolescent years they coalesce around their heroes and causes, their unity reinforced by the hostility of the larger society.

Almost everything about the young people of the sixties presented a blatant challenge to their elders: their long hair, dirty jeans, peace symbols, drug addiction, and sexual permissiveness. Their behavior was interpreted as an assault on patriotism; the work ethic, self-discipline, and other cherished adult values.

When you enter a town look as repulsive as you can.

—A motorcycle gang chieftain in the 1960s

Criticized and denounced by the older generation, the young people were drawn ever closer, seeing themselves as a victimized minority, a band apart, *us* and *them*. Seeking refuge, they retreated into their own taverns, dancehalls, and neighborhoods where those over thirty were never seen.

Don't trust anyone over thirty.

—Youth saying of the 1960s

In most small-scale societies the young and the old spend their hours in each other's company, but in the America of the sixties many of the young and the old walked away from each other so that not one but two new subcultures were born. The elders also developed a sense of group awareness and a consciousness of common problems. They too began to withdraw into their own social space by building "adult" communities which were restricted to their peers. Contrasting their own lives with the young people's they sometimes made use of a special language studded with such phrases as *If they would ever take a bath! If they would only learn to spell! If they would only cut their hair!*

Among the young people the subculture of youth became the antithesis of the predominant culture. Doing your own thing was lauded over self-discipline, "tripping" over studying, spontaneousness over uptightness, and indulgence over self-denial. Sexual inhibition was countered by promiscuity, alcoholism by drug addiction, and hard-nosed practicality by quixotic idealism. The subculture had become a counterculture.

Life Style How were the participants in the counterculture to be identified? Youth was not enough. Millions of young people—4H Club members, junior leaguers, fraternity brothers, sorority sisters, YMCA and YWCA members—never joined but remained firmly anchored in the larger American culture. For them the "Rock of Ages" signified something far more than "rock." If the followers of the counterculture were to distinguish themselves from conventional young people, they had to cultivate a life style of their own.

One way a life style expresses itself is in outward appearance. Each life style has its own wardrobe. Packed with General Grant tunics, broad-brimmed Australian rancher hats, Apache headbands, and frayed bleached shorts, as well as amulets, beads, badges, and joss sticks, the wardrobe of the counterculture clearly set its members apart from the "straight" world. A gathering of the youth tribe looked like a crowd of Hollywood extras on location. Young people traveled as never before and wherever they wandered the style went along with them. In Nepal, barefoot, clad in pajama bottoms and cotton vests, they dogged the heels of tourists peddling hashish, Gurka knives, and human skulls.

To the conventional, the new life style signaled the breakdown of order and tradition. For the followers of the counterculture, however, it was adaptive, helping them get by in a hostile world. It was a symbol of reliability and commitment, telling them who their friends were and who could be asked for a reefer, a loan, or a bed for the night. International in scope, whether in Canada, India, or Germany, the life style was an introduction to other members of the clan. It was a credit card and a card of identity.

Costume is only one part of a life style, which also includes values, outlook on life, feelings, and tastes. As much as any other manifestation of the youth style, rock music represented the ideals and manners of the counterculture. A battering ram that shook the values of the elders, breathless and brittle, insistent on beat and vibration, and tearing at the nerves, it swept away romanticism, sentimentality, and conventional musical composition. The lyrics, highly irreverent, held the sentiments of the older generation up to absurdity; love was translated into "Gimme gravy for my mashed potatoes." In thousands of homes Father yelled, "Will you turn that damn thing down."

The offensiveness of the music was magnified by the offensiveness of the performers who were often long haired, drug addicted, and tattered, or clothed in black-leather sequinned jackets and dark sun glasses. The audiences that came together in vast outdoor festivals where drugs were openly sold and young people took off their clothes added to the dismay of the older generation. Possibly no other culture, industrial or small scale, has ever expressed its ideals as vividly in music.

> Rock and Roll gets right through to you without having to go through your brain.
>
> —*John Lennon, once of the Beatles*

The Activists The counterculture was only one aspect of the youth movement of the sixties. In marked contrast to the alienated, hedonistic, and passive drug-addicted groups were the young people who remained in school and who attempted to influence the course of community and national life. These

In the midst of the youth movement of the 1960s most young people remained square. Rather than drop out into apathy or drugs, young activists sought to reform existing political and social conditions by organizing civil rights campaigns, peace groups, and environmental drives.

were the activists, the high school and college students who organized protests against the Indo-China war, worked on voter registration, rang doorbells, made speeches in national and local political campaigns, and spearheaded the civil rights movement in the South where some of them lost their lives. For a short time these young people became the conscience of America.

For young people to feel alienated and estranged is part of the experience of growing up in Western society. Also characteristic of adolescence is a sense of powerfulness, a feeling that anything is possible in this world whether it is improving oneself or creating a new order. Activism is as much a trait of the growing-up years as alienation.

Unlike the alienated, the activists of the sixties were not in rebellion against their parents' values but were attempting to breathe new life into traditional American ideals. Whatever was wrong could be corrected whether it was an irrelevant curriculum on campus, slum housing, or a war in Vietnam if only people of goodwill made up their minds and got busy. Although their resort to large-scale demonstrations and other direct action infuriated school administrators and the general public, their philosophy was firmly based on the sacred values of their country. Unlike the members of the counterculture, the activists discovered their greatest satisfactions not in the pursuit of pleasure or the exploration of inner vision but in the improvement of social and political life.

The Mainstream The youth movement, though it attracted tremendous national attention, never represented more than a minority of young people. Campus unrest was chiefly concentrated in a few universities such as Michigan, Cornell, Harvard, San Francisco State, and the University of California at Berkeley. Only 1–2 percent of college students were ever radical activists. Most youths remained in the mainstream, never doubting their place in the world their parents had made. Taking it for granted that they would graduate from school and find a suitable job and mate, they rejected neither money making, hard work, nor the competitive society. Politically moderate or conservative, they were absorbed in personal concerns such as popularity, sexual attractiveness, athletics, or allowances. Only when fellow students were shot down on the campus at Kent State or when they themselves were drafted for a war on the other side of the globe did some lose their "cool" and for a short time take up the standards of protest. Rebellion is not inevitable during adolescence. Even in the turbulent sixties millions of young people slipped quietly into adulthood. Cautious in outlook, mainstream youths nevertheless borrowed counterculture items such as long hair, T-shirts, faded jeans, and beads, although these had little influence on their daily behavior. They may have smoked marijuana, driven without a license, collected Mick Jagger records, and engaged in premarital sex; but they also admired their parents, stayed in school or held a steady job, and saved for the little house they would someday own in a good suburb. A few were Clark Kent infiltrators who on weekends merged with the "scene" but on Monday morning in jacket and tie quietly slipped back to class or the office. Unless it is a commitment to a whole system of values, a life style is only a fad to be shunted aside when a new one comes along.

The End of the Youth Movement Youth like every other stage in life is transitory. Young people cannot stay forever young. A youth crusade will not outlast a generation unless its cause remains. Even in the hectic sixties many young people had recognized that they would someday abandon the subculture they had created.

What they did not foresee was that the next generation of youth would not accept the torch from them. By the early seventies as the Vietnam war came to an end the youth movement disintegrated, living on only in a few isolated pockets and feeding on memories of a millennarian decade when it seemed to some that the young were about to change the manners and values of the nation. Haight-Ashbury in San Francisco, the East Village in New York, and other centers of the counterculture—once the Meccas of flower children, hippies, and runaways—lost their carnival atmosphere and again became dingy neighborhoods in great cities.

When the war in Vietnam ground to a halt, many of the activists felt that their mission had been accomplished and turned from politics to concentrate on their studies and careers. Many went into government, business, or the professions; a few were drawn into the women's liberation movement, religious sects, or tiny revolutionary groups. Some sought an alternative way of living by going back to the land. From Maine to the Ozarks long-haired youths migrated from the city to the countryside, reclaiming old farms, opening craft shops, or publishing weekly newspapers. Fleeing school or an office or factory job, they tried to live as simply as possible, relying on their own resources and producing as much as they could by themselves.

I went into the woods because I wanted to live deliberately, to front only the essential facts of life.

—*Henry Thoreau,* Walden, *1845*

I wanted to make my own beer, grow my own dope, and sleep with my own wife.

—*A young city migrant, Arkansas, 1975*

Like people in small-scale economies who depend on barter, the young migrants sought self-sufficiency by exchanging beans for wheat, milk for cheeses, or food stamps for sugar. Young people who could not have removed a washer back home embraced the work ethic and engaged in back-breaking labor from dawn to dusk, tilling the soil, milking cows, and restoring old barns. The back-to-the-land movement was characterized by values that many young people had rejected in the sixties: hard work, optimism, and a sense that everything is possible in this world. At the same time, unlike their parents who continued to hold down a regular job and dream of a day when they would at last retire to a condominium in Florida or a little house and garden in the country, these young people sought to taste and smell the good life immediately.

They're back to being kids again instead of political theorists and activists. It's refreshing to see young people acting like young people again.

—*An American high school teacher, 1975*

In the schools passivity replaced the early enthusiasm for snatching campus power from the administration. The stress was no longer on changing society but on individual ambition. Engrossed in goals and grades, a new generation of students concentrated on their studies and careers. Getting out the vote, going on hunger strikes, or occupying the dean's office gave way to Roller Skating Day, Groucho Marx festivals, beer busts, and beauty pageants. Dress still consisted of torn jeans and dirty sweatshirts, but it was no longer a symbol of revolt especially since the faculty was also dressing informally. For the most part teachers and parents were highly pleased. Political upheaval had given way to frivolity and studies.

I've heard about the troubles of the past years but I didn't come down here to prove anything except that I can have a good time. Most of the college kids I know don't have but two problems—getting a job when they get out of school and finding a place on this beach where you can have a little privacy with a girl.

—An American college student at Fort Lauderdale, Florida, 1977

The elders who had been so much concerned about the future of the country could have spared themselves a great deal of concern. A complex society can usually not only withstand the pressures generated by a subculture but also adapt those pressures to its purposes. At no time did the young rebels pose a real threat to the larger society. Given to conspicuous consumption like their parents, the young were a prop to the economy, an enormous army of consumers who spend over ten billion dollars a year and provided a new market for such products of the industrial system as clothing, motorcycles, surfboards, Volkswagens, stereos, guitars, and waterbeds. Underwritten by major corporations and marketed by shrewd promoters in long hair, rock 'n roll, once a cry of defiance, became a mainstay of television and radio. "That damn thing" became respectable. If the youth culture had not come into being, American industry might have been forced to invent it.

The diffusion of elements of the counterculture spread from youth to the elders. The regalia, marijuana, and sexual freedom that the conventional had rejected with loathing in the sixties became, if not respectable, at least tolerable in the seventies. Commerce waved its magic wand over the nation and counterculture costume became conformist garb. The establishment smoothly absorbed the surface elements of the youth movement and made them serve the economic and social interests of the society.

Though it may at times achieve an appearance of independence, a youth culture must change with the needs of the society that shelters it. It is an adaptation not only to the psychological drives of young people as they grow toward adulthood but also to the social and economic imperatives of the nation. Young people's dreams, fears, passions, enthusiasms, and manners, even their chronic unrest, are the arenas in which the general culture reveals itself. The youths who were hooked on "speed," LSD, or cocaine were often the children of parents who could not go through a twenty-four-hour period without recourse to tranquilizers, pain killers, sleeping pills, tobacco, or liquor. When some young rebels turned from drugs to alcohol, they eventually sought relief, like their fathers and mothers, in Alcoholics Anonymous.

A microcosm of the larger society, a youth culture may be symptomatic of trends not yet clearly articulated by the older generation. In the sixties at a time when young people seemed most isolated from the adult world, they were sounding some of the issues that would trouble their America in the years ahead: the status of women, sexual freedom, environmental destruction, loss of faith in political leaders.

> In youth . . . no longer is it merely for the old to teach the young the meaning of life. . . . It is the young who by their responses and actions tell the old whether life as represented by the old and as presented to the young has meaning.
>
> —*Erik Erikson, American psychiatrist, 1963*

In a world where very little can be known about tomorrow, youth scouts ahead and signals back the dangers that lie in wait. Less disturbed than the elders by departures from the norms of the culture, the younger generation may become an early warning system sensitive to the problems emerging in the larger society. Youth possesses the gift of prophecy.

In the last chapter we look in on the anthropologists, the people who study culture. How do they work? What are they after? What are their values?

the anthropologist and his work

15

"Where Is There a Tribe for Me?"

NAPOLEON A. CHAGNON, the American anthropologist, tells us how he first met the Yanomamö, a tribe he was to study for a good many years.

He arrived by boat at the Indian village on a very hot and muggy day. His clothing clung to his body; his hands and face were swollen with gnat bites. As he walked up the path toward the village and heard the buzz of activity within the compound, his heart began to pound. He was about to meet his first tribal people. Would they like him? Would they accept him? He was fully aware of their reputation for rage and ferocity. Pushing aside the brush that barred the entrance to the village, he waddled through the low passage into the clearing.

"I looked up and gasped when I saw a dozen burly naked filthy hideous men staring at us down the shafts of their drawn arrows. Immense wads of green tobacco were stuck between their lower teeth and lips making them look more hideous . . . there were a dozen or so vicious underfed dogs snapping at my legs circling me as though I was going to be their next meal . . . the stench of the decaying vegetation and filth struck me and I almost got sick . . . what sort of a welcome was this for a person who came here to live with you and learn your way of life, to become friends with you?"*

What was Chagnon doing so far from home, exposing himself to great discomfort, illness, and possible physical violence in the jungles of Venezuela? It was a question that he would frequently ask himself in his first days among the Yanomamö.

An anthropologist is a scientific investigator of culture who uses the tribal setting as other scientists use their laboratory. He studies his subject by means of systematic and objective observation, living among the people he has selected for his work, questioning them about their customs and institutions, and often taking part in their daily routines. In other words he does field work.

Field work provides the information on which anthropological conclusions are based. As much as he is able, the anthropologist participates in village life. Rather than setting up his own household, he may move in with a family, sleeping in their house, sharing their food, and joining in their festivals so that he may learn about their way of life through direct observation. Fortunately, tribal peoples are often quite hospitable toward (and curious about) the stranger who has come to stay with them accompanied by his cameras, tape recorders, two-way radios, insect repellents, mosquito netting, canned food, halting grammar, and impertinent questions. However, the hearty welcome may wear thin after a while, especially if the anthropologist has failed to provide himself with a plentiful supply of gifts and his own source of food.

Sometimes, instead of scurrying after the hunters and frightening off all the game in the vicinity, the anthropologist will stay close to the heart of the community in order to interview informants and observe what is going on. Informants are members of the community who supply the anthropologist with information about such matters as kinship relations, taboos,

*Yanomamö the Fierce People by Napoleon A. Chagnon. New York: Holt, Rinehart and Winston, 1968, p. 5.

witchcraft beliefs, sexual behavior, values, and myths. A good informant may also become the anthropologist's language teacher.

An anthropologist may begin his research by finding out who is related to whom. He knows that in a small-scale community social life is based on kinship relations. He may then proceed to gather data on births, deaths, marriages, residence patterns, inventories of personal property, and trade patterns within the village.

The techniques the anthropologist uses and the way he uses them will be related to the purposes of his research. Long before he steps into the village he knows what questions he wants answered and what hypotheses he wants to test. He is not in the field merely to absorb strange customs and ways of life, but to engage in scientific research.

The Anthropologist As Interpreter Let us suppose that the anthropologist wants to understand the relations of men and women in a lowland South American Indian community. For his study he selects a small isolated village along the Xingu River in the heart of Brazil. Soon after his arrival he notices that the men and the women, like the sexes all over the world, perform different tasks. In this community the men fish, hunt, build houses, make canoes, and clear the ground for planting manioc. The principal food of the Xingu region, manioc is a starchy root plant that looks somewhat like an overgrown turnip. The variety these people raise is poisonous. Before it can be used for food, it must be scraped, ground, and squeezed—a time-consuming and arduous task that is assigned to the women. The women also take care of the household and the children, cook, weave hammocks, and make the manioc flour for bread.

The anthropologist turns to a female informant and asks a deliberately simple question: "Why is it that the women of your village don't do the fishing?"

"Now what would women be doing in the hot sun?" she replies, amazed at the naiveté of the white man. "It is the men

In many tribal societies the roles of men and women are separated far more than in Western societies. • In a Xingu Indian village it would be unthinkable that a woman should fish, just as it would be outrageous that a man should weave a hammock. Left, a Xingu male uses a fish trap. Right, a Xingu female weaves a hammock.

who fish, not the women, and that is as it has been since the days of our ancestors." And so say many other villagers. "Tradition tells us that men and women have separate tasks."

The anthropologist, however, quickly becomes aware that reliance on tradition is not enough to keep men and women to their assigned work. The villagers are constantly resorting to sanctions, that is, rewards and penalties, to make certain that people abide by the sexual division of labor. A female who tried the male specialty of weaving a basket would be mocked and called a fool. A man who broke with tradition by taking on the woman's task of making a hammock would be derided and called a woman. People are so timorous of taking on a task assigned to one sex that a husband will wait for hours for his wife to come home to bake bread rather than do it himself.

Why are the sanctions that enforce the sexual division of labor so strong in this village? The anthropologist has already observed that manioc is a staple of the Xinguano diet and that its

production demands the services of both men and women. The men clear the fields for the planting of manioc, but the women harvest it, turn it into flour, and then into bread. Its production depends on the mutual exchange of male and female labor.

A pattern of sharply different sex roles appears to pervade the entire life of the Xingu community. The anthropologist comes across this division not only in food production but in family life, politics, etiquette, and religion. Men and women frequent different parts of the village. Women spend much of their time in the back of the houses; men congregate on the plaza in front of the houses. Women are completely barred from entering the men's house, a combined religious and recreational center where the males conduct the business of the village. A woman who dared to spy on activities conducted in the men's house would be subject to severe punishment.

From his background reading, the anthropologist knows that a drastic degree of separation of the men and women—far greater than that in Western society—is typical of small-scale communities such as the Xingu village. Such strict separation is apparently related to the environment in which the people live and to the level of their technology. In a tribal group such vital tasks as warfare, hunting, and clearing the land can be conducted more efficiently when done by men. A sharp division of labor between men and women may provide an adaptive advantage in a society that relies on simple tools for work.

The anthropologist has begun by observing the relations of men and women, but he soon discovers that if he is to understand such a relation he must link it to the total life style. A custom makes sense only when it is fitted into an entire culture. An architect is not going to learn very much about the structure of an igloo by study of each individual ice block. What he must discover is the structural principle used to fit one block to another. The anthropologist may be fascinated by the customs of the people he is studying, but he is also interested in the way these customs interrelate to make a consistent culture. An observer and interviewer, he is also an interpreter, searching for the organization that holds a human society together.

Cultural Relativism Soon after arriving at his village, the field worker, especially if he is new at the game as Chagnon was, is likely to be overwhelmed by culture shock, a feeling of anxiety that is often accompanied by depression and loneliness. Despite his training and his preparation for his work, he may feel hostility and irritation toward people about whom he should feel only scientific objectivity. Thousands of miles from home, cut off from friends and family, usually white, middle class, and university educated, he may experience a sense of revulsion toward tribal people whose habits of eating, sleeping, toileting, and cleanliness are so very different from his. What troubled Chagnon most on his first visit to the Yanomamö was the lack of privacy and the Indians' endless demands for almost everything he had brought with him.

At this stage in field work the anthropologist must turn to a study of himself. To what extent are his ideas of what is mine and what is yours, of what is clean and dirty, of what is right and wrong, of what is decent and indecent—in short, his ethnocentrism—getting in the way of appreciating the life ways of his hosts? Bronislaw Malinowski, one of the first anthropologists to do field work among tribal peoples, kept a secret diary in which he vented his feelings toward the Trobriand Islanders who sheltered him. By admitting his repugnance and hostility to himself, he managed to keep such feelings from hindering his understanding of the people he was studying.

Once he emerges from his culture shock, the anthropologist may be ready to judge the people among whom he is working not by his Western standards but by theirs, a point of view sometimes called cultural relativism. He begins to appreciate that this strange and alien way of life may be as valid a scheme for dealing with the problems of human existence and welfare as the one from which he happens to come. He learns to evaluate the life style of the people by the way it evolves and differentiates, by the manner in which its elements interrelate, and by the advantages or disadvantages it confers on its population. He tries to see others as they see themselves. Emphasizing the worthwhileness of other cultures, cultural relativism respects the right of every people to adhere to their own beliefs and behavioral patterns.

Do not judge a man until you have walked three days in his moccasins.

—*Saying attributed to the American Plains Indians*

Cultural relativism does not require that the anthropologist become an apologist for the society he is studying. To see only harmony and generosity in a small-scale community and only disorder and selfishness in his own would be no guide to scientific truth. No society is the chosen people. All cultures are local and eventually pass away.

How close can the anthropologist draw to *his* tribe without harming his professional integrity? The early American anthropologist Frank Hamilton Cushing in the course of his long stay among the Zuni was adopted by a family and became a chief of the tribe. Apparently because of his allegiance to his new people he withheld valuable material from publication. Despite admiration for his people, an anthropologist should never go native. He must always remain an outsider.

Never can the anthropologist feel himself at home anywhere; he will always be, psychologically speaking, an amputee.

—Claude Lévi-Strauss

Because every culture is unique, each must be judged in terms of its own values. For Chagnon to upbraid a Yanomamö father for needling his son to strike him would be as pointless as for a Yanomamö to criticize American parent-child relationships. Chagnon had come all the way from Michigan not to teach the inhabitants of the Venezuelan jungle how to live but to learn their ways of life from them. Chagnon was not among the Yanomamö long before he realized that in a society in which a fierce disposition helps to keep a man alive, a father who did not cultivate aggression in his son would be failing in his duty.

Yet cultural relativism does raise dilemmas for the field worker. Is he expected to be so objective that he accepts all customs with equal impartiality, no matter how cruel and inhuman they may seem to him? Suppose he is living with a hunting and gathering band that abandons the aged and the crippled to perish alone in the wilderness. Must he refrain from being shocked? Probably not. At the same time he can understand that where survival depends on following the trail of migratory game, stopping for those who cannot keep up with the line of march could cause the death of the entire band. Though he need not endorse customs that are abhorrent to him, he tries to see them in the light of the entire community's needs.

The Anthropologist at Home The anthropologist is a student not only of simple societies but also of his own. Having developed his skills in a remote corner of the earth, he will often turn to a study of other cultures, including his own. It is understandable that the young anthropologist should cut his eyeteeth in field work in small-scale communities.

Compared to a simple culture the United States might seem impossible to comprehend. Divided into urban, suburban, and rural settlements the country exhibits not one but dozens of life styles. Socially and economically it is organized not around kin but schools, factories, labor unions, and government bureaucracies. Just attempting to list a core of common values on which all Americans can agree is a task on which social scientists have floundered. How fascinatingly clear and simple a tribal or peasant community must seem in comparison with an industrial nation.

Historically, anthropology has emphasized the study of small-scale societies. In the nineteenth century England, France, and the other great colonial powers had carved out empires in Africa, Asia, Australia, and the South Pacific, the homelands of many tribal peoples. To the colonial powers anthropologists, like missionaries, were a useful source of information about the native populations they sought to control. Anthropology became a study not so much of all humanity, but of colored peoples living in nonindustrial societies in primitive regions of the world.

The game, however, has changed. Fleeing the rising tide of nationalism around the earth, the colonial powers have fallen back to their home bases in Europe. Many thousands of tribal communities have disappeared as though they never existed. Others, acculturated by contact with the West, have abandoned their original way of life. So, although anthropologists can still be found working in the few tribal societies comparatively uninfluenced by the West, many of them are turning for their field work to societies that are in the process of change or already in the mainstream of contemporary technological development. In a recent Broadway musical comedy, a young woman anthropologist plaintively sings, "Where is there a tribe for me?" The answer, she discovers, is at home as she turns for her research to a band of gypsies occupying a storefront on her own street.

At home the anthropologist may find his society as exciting as any he encountered in the desert or jungle, for the study of industrial cultures can be as rewarding for the understanding of humans as that of the Eskimo or Arunta. As well as tribal peoples, Americans have their taboos, rites of passage, legends, ceremonials, kinship systems, values—the full range of learned behavior common to people everywhere. The anthropologist, however, will generally leave to other social scientists a total survey of an industrial culture. Instead, he tends to focus on aspects of Western society in which he can be both a participant and an observer. Field work is based on face-to-face experience. If he is studying American culture he may select a subject such as race relations in a minority community, folk speech in a rural setting, family reunions, new religious movements, a comparison of values in two communities, or social life in a large city.

Applied Anthropology We live in a world where Westernization is obliterating differences among people. As the speed of communication increases, native cultures disintegrate, overwhelmed by contact with the goods and ideas of the great industrial nations. Where the helicopter casts its shadow people soon begin to consume the same packaged foods, listen to the same music, drink the same bottled sodas, wear the same clothing, and subscribe to the same values. Deep in the wild Mato Grosso of Brazil young Indian youths go about with transistors to their ears, listening to current song hits coming from a radio station in Rio de Janeiro a thousand miles away.

Tribal cultures that still remain relatively intact provide us with an assortment of models for human behavior. Social laboratories, they are living illustrations of the cultural inventiveness of the human race. Each one constitutes a precious experiment that can never be tried again. Wherever they possibly

Well-meaning projects intended to improve the life of people in underdeveloped countries may founder because the planners have failed to consider the people's tastes and values. In central Tanzania, Africa, a pilot nutrition program tried, with great difficulty, to introduce fish into the local diet. The natives rejected fish at first because "They're slippery like snakes." After three years of intensive education by the Food and Agriculture Organization, these Tanzanians finally came to enjoy fish prepared with curry and tomatoes.

Unlike the anthropologist who interferes as little as possible with a society's way of life while studying it, the applied anthropologist deliberately sets out to create a particular change in a community. Working with an organization such as the Food and Agricultural Organization of the United Nations, he assists in the modernization of traditional and inefficient ways of farming. • A group of farmers in the Central African Republic listen to a radio agricultural extension course.

can, anthropologists, therefore, are trying to keep a number of small-scale communities alive not only for humanitarian but for scientific reasons.

One of the important fields of study amog anthropologists today is cultural change. An anthropologist may want to preserve native cultures, but he must acknowledge that almost all of them are changing rapidly. In what is termed "applied anthropology" the field worker does not merely study changes as they occur but assists in the introduction of programs in underdeveloped areas such as child care, public sanitation, nutrition, and education. Working in conjunction with organizations such as the Peace Corps or the United Nations, the applied anthropologist deliberately involves himself in planned cultural innovations and uses his scientific skills to help tribal and peasant peoples solve some of the critical problems that confront them in a changing world.

There is still another task to which the anthropologist can address himself. Can the insights he has drawn from his study of other cultures contribute to helping his own? Despite its vast scientific and technological progress, contemporary civilization sometimes appears to be an aberrant form of evolution, a mass culture bent on its own destruction. Every culture is an adaptation to its social and physical environment; yet every culture contains within itself lethal elements that can bring about its extinction.

As a student of human behavior can the anthropologist help us discover alternative attitudes that will build rather than destroy the natural environment? Can he help us solve the economic and ecological puzzle that will send 60 percent of humanity to bed hungry tonight? Can he address himself to the destructive aspects of human behavior that allow an airman who is a model citizen at home to release a bomb that obliterates a city abroad, or that encourages a housewife who would not harm a pet to press a torture button?

> We have come seriously to consider ourselves as possibly one kind of living creature in a universe that may contain many other kinds of living creatures possibly more intelligent than ourselves. This possibility adds new zest to the exploration of our own potentialities as members of one species entrusted with the preservation of an endangered world. . . .
>
> —*Margaret Mead*

Anthropology is an exciting and adventurous profession, though the commitment is not to the adventure or the excite-

Can the anthropologist's study of human behavior in all its manifestations contribute to the solution of some crucial problems that trouble industrial societies throughout the world—problems such as the unequal distribution of resources, the threat of devastating war, or the deterioration of the natural environment? • Pollution over Westfalenhuette, near Dortmund in West Germany.

ment but to the scientific analysis that allows us to recognize in all cultures "the coexisting and equally valid patterns of life which mankind has created for itself from the raw materials of existence." In the behavior of a distant star the astronomer discovers the secrets of his own sun. In a remote land the anthropologist finds himself at home again.

glossary

acculturation behavior changes of a people who come into contact with a more powerful society and thus acquire many of its cultural elements

achieved status social position occupied by a person as a result of his own abilities and effort

activism philosophy of life dependent on vigorous action and involvement

adaptation process by which a people copes with the social and physical environment in order to survive

adolescence stage in life extending from onset of puberty to attainment of full reproductive maturity

age set group of persons of similar age and sex who move through the stages of life together

angakok Eskimo shaman

apocalyptic referring to the end of the world as revealed in religious prophecy

applied anthropology application of anthropological knowledge to influence social institutions or bring about cultural change

ascribed status social position assigned to a person without regard to his ability or efforts such as those based on age or sex

band small hunting and gathering group, usually nomadic, sharing a common territory; size varies with availability of food

berdache Plains American Indian transvestite who assumed female social role

bull roarer slatted piece of wood which produces a roaring noise when whirled about on the end of a string

Cargo cult revivalist movement in Melanesia asserting that a ship or plane would soon arrive laden with European goods and ancestors returned from the dead

caste closed social group whose members marry only among themselves, often linked to a particular occupation as in India

charismatic referring to a divinely conferred gift such as the ability to speak in tongues, drive out demons, or heal spiritually

circumcision surgical removal of the foreskin of the penis; often performed during a puberty ceremony

civilization relatively high level of technological development; specifically stage at which writing and written words occur
clan kinship group supposedly descended from a common ancestor
community largest group of people who know each other on a face-to-face basis, inhabit a common territory, and share a system of communication and a feeling of belongingness
conjugal referring to relation between husband and wife
consanguineous related by blood, having the same ancestry
coup deed of courage among the American Plains Indians
couvade practice in which a husband mimics his wife's pregnancy and delivery
cross-cousins children of siblings of the opposite sex such as my father's sister's children or my mother's brother's children
cross-cultural referring to comparisons between two or more cultures
cult organized group which has a special set of beliefs and supernatural rituals
culture patterns of thought, feeling, and behavior acquired through learning; a life style
diffusion process by which cultural elements are borrowed by one culture from another
ecology study of the relationship between organisms (including humans) and their total environment
enculturation process by which a person assimilates the elements of his culture; also called socialization
endogamy rule requiring a person to marry within his own social group or community
ethnocentrism belief that the customs of outsiders should be judged in terms of one's own culture; belief in the superiority of one's own culture
exogamy practice or requirement that one marry outside his own social group
extended family kinship group that includes near relatives in addition to parents and their offspring
family kinship group consisting minimally of a married couple and their immature offspring
genealogy study of family ancestries
glossolalia incomprehensible speech in the course of ecstatic worship; called "speaking in tongues"

group marriage marriage of several males and several females; very rare
hogan Navajo Indian home
incest sexual contact between close relatives
infanticide practice in some societies of killing infants
invention alteration or combination of materials, procedures, or practices to produce a new form of material or activity; in contrast to a discovery, which is the recognition of something already in existence but of which people had been previously unaware
kachina god of the Hopi Indians whom masked dancers impersonate in a rain dance
kibbutz communal settlement in Israel, usually agricultural
kiva underground ceremonial chamber of the Hopi Indians
life style culture of a society or of one of its subgroups
magic control of natural forces by such means as spells or amulets
marriage union of two or more persons which regulates their relations to each other, their offspring, kinsmen, and society
matricentric family household headed by a woman whose husband is absent or only rarely present; also called matrifocal
millennial referring to a future time of righteousness and happiness
monogamy marriage in which a person has only one spouse at a time
myth legendary story concerning the supernatural and its effects on human beings which offers explanations of natural phenomena, of how things came to be, and of human behavior
natal family kinship group into which a person is born
nuclear family kinship group consisting of parents and their immature offspring
occult referring to magic, astrology, and other aspects of the supernatural; hidden, mysterious
parallel cousins children of siblings of the same sex such as the children of my father's brother or my mother's sister
peasants rural people who produce food for their own use and trade their surpluses to city and town dwellers
Pentecostal referring to Christian churches and rituals in which religious feelings are expressed without inhibition
plural marriage marriage of more than two spouses at a time
polyandry marriage in which a woman has two or more husbands at the same time

polygamy practice of having several spouses at one time
polygyny marriage in which a man has two or more wives at once
potlatch ceremonial feast among Northwest Coast Indians marked by lavish distribution of gifts and in a later time by destruction of wealth
priest full-time religious functionary whose authority is derived from a church or cult in contrast to the shaman whose power is said to be acquired from the supernatural
primitive referring to a culture without a written language and possessing only a simple technology
puberty rite rite of passage that ushers young people out of childhood nearer to or into adulthood
reciprocity mutual exchange of goods without calculation of the advantages to either side
religion practices, attitudes and beliefs relating to supernatural beings and forces
revitalization reform religious movement which appears at times of severe stress such as colonial conquest of the Pacific Islanders or the American Indians; sometimes also described as millennarian, revivalist, nativistic, or messianic
rites of passage ceremonies associated with important changes in status such as those of birth, adolescence, or marriage
ritual established or prescribed procedure for performance of ceremonial acts
role behavior associated with a particular occupation or status such as that of parent, student, priest, or chief
sacred referring to the out of the ordinary; also refers to that which is entitled to veneration because of association with the supernatural
sanction authorization or support for an action; penalty or reward for a particular behavior
seclusion period of isolation during which a person lives apart from the daily life of his society, as in the course of a change of status
sex role behavior expected of a person because of his or her sex
sexual division of labor assignment of work on the basis of sex
shaman part-time religious specialist with an inborn gift for manipulating supernatural power in order to heal, predict the future,

find lost objects, or otherwise affect the course of natural events

small-scale society small, homogeneous, and self-sufficient community that possesses a simple technology; also called a simple or primitive society

socialization acquisition of patterns of behavior acceptable to one's culture; also called enculturation

society group of people who possess a distinct culture, a sense of common interests, and social and economic interdependence

sorcery attempt to harm people using medicines and other materials to manipulate supernatural forces; black magic

spirit possession control of a person by a supernatural being

status social position that a person occupies within his group

supernatural that which is unexplainable by natural law, such as gods and spirits

superstition belief in the ominous significance of an event or thing not based on reason or knowledge; used sometimes to refer to religious beliefs other than one's own

syncretic referring to the merging of originally different or opposing beliefs and practices, as occurs in new religions

taboo rule which if broken subjects its violator to automatic and supernatural punishment

technology cultural knowledge required to make and use tools and machinery; means by which a society provides the material objects of its culture

totem pole post carved and painted with mythological figures by Northwest Coast Indians; post proclaims the rank and power of its possessor

tribe group larger than a band whose members have a common language, territory, and name

value standards of personal and social conduct about which people have strong feelings

witch person born with supernatural power who uses it for evil purposes

witch doctor African shaman who protects his clients against witchcraft

youth stage in life between attainment of reproductive maturity and the beginning of adulthood

further reading

(Almost all books listed are in paperback. Those marked with an asterisk are suggested for the beginning reader in anthropology.)

Alland, Alexander, Jr. *The Human Imperative.* New York: Columbia University Press, 1972.
Conflict and war are not an inescapable part of our biology.

Barnouw, Victor. *Culture and Personality.* Homewood, Ill.: Dorsey Press, 1973.
A number of social scientists view the problems of culture and personality.

Benedict, Ruth. *Patterns of Culture.* New York: New American Library, 1959.*
Though subject to correction, still one of the most entrancing studies of the meaning hidden behind culture.

Biocca, Ettore. *Yanóama: The Narrative of a White Girl Kidnapped by Amazonian Indians.* New York: E. P. Dutton, 1970.*
Helena Valero's true story of living among the Yanomamö Indians for twenty years. High adventure and good anthropology.

Bodley, John H. *Victims of Progress.* Menlo Park, Ca.: Cummings Publishing Co., 1975.
Description of tribal people living in today's world.

Bohonnan, Paul. *Africa and Africans.* Garden City, N.Y.: Natural History Press, 1964.
Quick survey of the varied peoples of Africa.

Brandon, William. *The American History Book of Indians.* New York: Dell Publishing Co., 1971.
Short history of the American Indians from the earliest times.

Brown, Dee. *Bury My Heart at Wounded Knee.* New York: Holt, Rinehart and Winston, 1971.*
As the Indians saw the conquest of the West.

Brown, Claude. *Manchild in the Promised Land.* New York: New American Library, 1965.
A black adolescent growing up in a city slum.

Brown, Ina Corinne. *Understanding Other Cultures.* Englewood Cliffs, N.J.: Prentice-Hall, 1965.*

Gentle examination of the way different societies have met the problems of living in the world.

Castaneda, Carlos. *The Teachings of Don Juan.* New York: Simon and Schuster, 1968.*

Fledgling anthropologist becomes shaman's apprentice and gives up his critical faculties. Fascinating and unbelievable.

Chagnon, Napoleon A. *Yanomamö, the Fierce People.* New York: Holt, Rinehart and Winston, 1968.

Stirring account of an anthropologist's stay among a dangerous people.

Cohn, Norman. *Europe's Inner Demons.* St. Albans, Eng.: Paladin Books, 1976.

The great witch hunts of the fifteenth through seventeenth centuries.

Collier, John. *Indians of the Americas.* New York: New American Library, 1947.*

Fascinating account by the former Commissioner of Indian Affairs. Eloquent and moving.

Cooper, John Charles. *Religion in the Age of Aquarius.* Philadelphia: Westminster Press, 1971.*

A glimpse at new religious trends in America including the occult explosion.

Deloria, Vine, Jr. *Custer Died for Your Sins.* New York: Macmillan, 1969.

Story of the Indians in the contemporary world.

Dentan, Robert Knox. *The Semai, a Nonviolent People of Malaya.* New York: Holt, Rinehart and Winston, 1962.

Anthropological report about a people who refuse to be aggressive.

Douglas, Jack D. *Youth in Turmoil.* Rockville, Md.: National Institute of Mental Health, 1972.

Balanced view of the youth subcultures of the 1960s.

Durkheim, Emile. *The Elementary Forms of the Religious Life.* New York: Collier Books, 1961.

Religion among the Australian aborigines. A classic.

Elliot, Katherine (Ed.). *The Family and Its Future.* London: J. and A. Churchill, 1970.

The experts talk about what the future holds in store for today's Western family.

Erikson, Erik H. (Ed.). *Youth: Change and Challenge.* New York: Basic Books, 1961.
Psychologists and psychiatrists on the problems of youth.

Ford, Clellan S., and Beach, Frank A. *Patterns of Sexual Behavior.* New York: Harper and Row, 1951.
Everything you ever wanted to know about sexual behavior, human and nonhuman. Sound and scholarly.

Fox, Robin. *Kinship and Marriage.* New York: Penguin Books, 1970.
An authoritative, concise account.

Frazer, Sir James. *The Golden Bough.* New York: Macmillan, 1947.*
Survey of strange customs, legends, myths all over the globe. Be sure to at least skim through it.

Fried, Morton (Ed.). *War: the Anthropology of Armed Conflict and Aggression.* Garden City, N.Y.: Natural History Press, 1968.
The character and causes of tribal warfare by leading authorities.

Goffman, Erving. *The Presentation of Self in Everyday Life.* Garden City, N.Y.: Anchor Books, 1959.
Fascinating analysis of our everyday behavior.

Golde, Peggy (Ed.). *Women in the Field.* Chicago: Aldine, 1970.
No male monopoly, anthropology; women tell of their field work.

Harris, Marvin. *Cows, Pigs, Wars and Witches: The Riddles of Culture.* New York: Random House, 1974.*
Why do people behave as they do? Harris has some answers. Delightful reading.

Harris, Marvin. *Cannibals and Kings: The Origins of Culture.* New York: Random House, 1977.*
Harris back with more solutions.

Henry, Jules. *Culture against Man.* New York: Vintage Books, 1963.
A critical view of American family life, schooling, and treatment of the aged and the mentally ill.

Henry, Jules. *Jungle People.* New York: Random House, 1964.
An anthropologist participates in the daily life of the fighting Kaingang Indians.

Herskowitz, Melville S. *Life in a Haitian Valley.* Garden City, N.Y.: Doubleday and Co., 1971.*
Rural life in Haiti with description of voodoo.

Hess, Stephen (Chairman). *Report of the White House Conference on Youth.* Washington, D.C.: Government Printing Office, 1971.
A thousand young people tell where they are at.

Horwitz, J., and Lanter, Elinor. *Communes in America.* Philadelphia: J. B. Lippincott, 1972.
A quick look at centuries of communes in America.

Hymes, Dell (Ed.). *Reinventing Anthropology.* New York: Pantheon Books, 1972.
Anthropologists do not all think alike; essays on a variety of subjects.

Kluckhohn, Clyde. *Mirror for Man.* Greenwich, Conn.: Fawcett Publications, 1944.*
Short account of what anthropology is and does.

Kroeber, Theodore. *Ishi in Two Worlds.* Berkeley, Calif.: University of California Press, 1961.*
If there were only one book I could recommend . . . discovery of the last Indian to live as his ancestors did.

Kuper, Hilda. *The Swazi: A South African Kingdom.* New York: Holt, Rinehart and Winston, 1963.
A way of life in a highly centralized African monarchy.

Lévi-Strauss, Claude. *Tristes Tropiques.* New York: Atheneum, 1967.*
Journey through the Brazilian wilds with a great anthropologist. Adventure and science.

Lewis, Oscar. *Five Families.* New York: Basic Books, 1959.
A typical day in the lives of five Mexican families.

Lewis, Oscar. *Tepoztlán: Village in Mexico.* New York: Holt, Rinehart and Winston, 1960.
Daily living in a Mexican village that is changing rapidly under the impact of Western culture.

Liebow, E. *Tally's Corner.* Boston: Little, Brown, 1967.
Anthropological field work in a Washington, D.C., ghetto.

Mair, Lucy. *Witchcraft.* New York: McGraw-Hill, 1971.
Witchcraft mostly in Africa and what people do about it.

Malinowski, Bronislaw. *Magic, Science, and Religion and Other Essays.* Boston: Beacon Press, 1948.
Emphasizes uncertainty as a source of religious feeling.

Marriott, Alice. *The Ten Grandmothers.* Norman, Okla.: University of Oklahoma Press, 1945.*
Kiowa Indian life as told by the people themselves.

Mead, Margaret. *People and Places.* New York: Bantam Books, 1959.*
How anthropologists study different societies.

Mead, Margaret. *Sex and Temperament in Three Primitive Societies.* New York: William Morrow, 1963.
Study of sex roles in three New Guinea tribes among whom Mead lived.

Middleton, John (Ed.). *Magic, Witchcraft and Curing.* Garden City, N.Y.: Natural History Press, 1967.
Informative articles by social scientists.

Middleton, John (Ed.). *From Child to Adult.* Garden City, N.Y.: Natural History Press, 1970.
Different societies, different types of education; articles by leading authorities.

Montagu, M. F. Ashley (Ed.). *Man and Aggression.* London: Oxford University Press, 1968.
Contributors demolish the alleged inborn aggressive drive of humans.

Pfeiffer, John E. *The Emergence of Society.* New York: McGraw-Hill, 1977.
Development of various societies, present-day and prehistorical.

Radin, Paul. *The World of Primitive Man.* New York: Grove Press, 1960.
Leaves the reader with new respect for tribal people.

Read, Kenneth E. *The High Valley.* New York: Charles Scribner's Sons, 1965.
A New Guinea tribe seen through the lives of several people.

Redfield, Robert. *The Primitive World and Its Transformations.* Ithaca, N.Y.: Cornell University Press, 1953.
A series of popular lectures summing up the differences between simple and complex societies.

Rozaldo, M. Z. (Ed.). *Woman, Culture and Society.* Stanford, Calif.: Stanford University Press, 1973.
Female anthropologists report on the status of women in various societies.

Service, Elman R. *Profiles in Ethnology.* New York: Harper and Row, 1958.
Brief descriptions of preliterate people such as the Zulu, Eskimo, Cheyenne, and Tahitians.

Spradley, James P. (Ed.). *Conformity and Conflict.* Boston: Little, Brown, 1971.
Readings in cultural anthropology that deal with tribal, peasant, and industrial cultures.

Thomas, Elizabeth Marshall. *The Harmless People.* New York: Vintage Books, 1959.*
We relive the author's life among the Kalahari Bushmen.

Turnbull, Colin M. *The Forest People.* New York: Anchor Books, 1961.*
The Ituri Forest Pygmies in Africa described so vividly that you tend to believe the author is a Pygmy.

Turnbull, Colin M. *The Lonely African.* New York: Anchor Books, 1962.
The changing lives of Africans as they leave their villages and become city dwellers.

Underhill, Ruth M. *First Came the Family.* New York: William Morrow, 1958.*
Contrasts kinship and family relations in America and in other societies.

Wagley, C. W. *An Introduction to Brazil.* New York: Columbia University Press, 1971.
Sums up Brazilian people and history.

Weyer, Edward, Jr. *Primitive People Today.* New York: Crescent Books, 1974.*
Brief sketches of fourteen tribal groups; striking photographs.

If you would like to try a textbook in general anthropology I would recommend: E. Adamson Hoebel, *Anthropology: The Study of Man* (New York: McGraw-Hill, 1966). It is authoritative, well organized, and clearly written. Also recommended is *Cultural Anthropology: A Contemporary Perspective* by Roger M. Keesing (New York: Holt, Rinehart and Winston, 1976).

On September 5, 1977, the National Aeronautics and Space Administration cast Voyager II *into outer space. It contained messages intended to give extraterrestrial beings perhaps millions of years later some idea of the peoples and cultures of planet Earth. Evidence of the human way of life included pictures of a microscope, a radio telescope, a rocket launching, and houses; recordings of greetings in fifty-five languages; the sounds made by a tractor, a train whistle, and a wood saw; and a sequence of music from Bach to Chuck Berry to a raga of India to a night chant of the Navajo. Should higher intelligences ever intercept* Voyager II, *will they be able to interpret the messages? Can evidence of human culture convey meaning to nonhuman beings—however far advanced?*

index